EDGE OF
TOMORROW

EDGE OF TOMORROW

An Arctic Year

SAM WRIGHT

Washington State University Press
Pullman, Washington

Washington State University Press
PO Box 645910
Pullman, Washington 99164-5910
Phone: 800-354-7360   FAX: 509-335-8568
©1998 by the Board of Regents of Washington State University
All rights reserved
First printing 1998

Cover photograph by Donna Lee.

Library of Congress Cataloging-in-Publication Data
Wright, Sam, 1919-
          Edge of tomorrow : an Arctic year / Sam Wright.
              p.   cm.—(Northwest voices essay series)
          ISBN 0-87422-167-6 (pbk.)
          1. Brooks Range (Alaska)—Description and travel.   2. Brooks Range
(Alaska)—Biography.   3. Seasons—Alaska—Brooks Range.
4. Wright, Sam, 1919-   .   I. Title.   II. Series.
          F912.B75W755   1998   98-24085
          979.8'7—dc21   CIP

To Stephen Hawking, Ken Kesey,
Madeline Albright, and others unknown
who live deliberately
on their edge of tomorrow.

I went to the woods because I wished to live deliberately, to front only the essential facts of life, and see if I could not learn what it had to teach, and not, when I came to die, discover that I had not lived.

—Henry David Thoreau, *Walden*

Contents

Introduction

A<small>N ALMANAC IS COMPOSED</small> of calendars and information in many unrelated fields including astronomical information and weather.

If weather has to do with the way the wind blows in the world of meaning, and astronomical information includes current cosmology, and if one's assumptions about such matters need continual revision, then this perspective from north of the Arctic Circle in the wilderness of the Brooks Range of Alaska is an almanac of exploration.

Today we are beginning to explore what it means to be part of a universe that is alive. We are discovering new versions of a lost world that was part of the natural mind for most of human history.

For many, this emerging view of nature is in a realm separate from the textures and emotions of daily experience. However, the insights of quantum physics and what has been called a new consciousness shift our assumptions about reality.

∾

All speculation about meaning is based upon our assumptions about reality.

One part of reality is what we call subjective. Another is objective. Objective is the reality out there. It is the "what is."

Subjective has to do with the way we create reality inside ourselves. We create reality out of our observations and our assumptions of the what is. It is what the "in here" does with the "out there" that makes our reality.

Our assumptions define the myths by which we live.

If we conceive of our assumptions as myths, they are no longer objective reality. Myths are the way we conceive, perceive, and organize our assumptions.

There is a paradox here. As soon as we perceive our reality to be mythic, it loses its connection with objective reality. It is then that we create a new sense of reality to which we are willing to commit ourselves. This commitment is our religion. This becomes the story, the tale, by which we live.

∽

Here is a tale of the way it is now, before the story becomes myth.

In the beginning there was no beginning. When I am told that the universe began with a big bang, I ask, as any child would, "What was before the big bang?"

When you think about it, there is nothing in our experience to affirm a beginning. Everything appears to come from something else. Plant from seed, seed from plant, water from gasses, gasses from atoms, atoms from quarks, and so on until we come full circle.

It is not difficult to think of no beginning if we think of change or transformation. What most people call beginnings are actually transformations.

My astronomer friends speak of the big bang as a "singularity" when they talk about beginning. However, I cannot conceive of singularity without thinking of multiplicity, and this produces in me a chuckle.

What is the nature of connections between a big bang theory and my chuckle? Somehow reality has roots here.

Am I serious? Is it a joke?

Although we may recognize that there is no beginning, we do pick up our story somewhere in this whereless universe of stars and life and mind. It is our story which creates reality out of the stuff of reality. The way we tell the story defines reality for us.

My story is not serious. Seriousness is a state of mind which denies ambiguity and paradox. From what we observe of the universe we know today, there is no way to rule out paradox or ambiguity. Humor deals with ambiguity. To see humor in anything is to touch the reality of it. As has been said, a human being who cannot laugh might as well be dead.

Whether you call it laughter or play, out of eons of transformation this sense of meaningful ambiguity has taken form in the human psyche. It is a window of mind through which we view the universe with a sense of adventure and joy.

$$\backsim$$

To write with any objectivity about a theology of nature, terms must be defined. In particular, the terms theology and nature. Nature is from the Latin *natura*, birth. It is conceived (no pun intended) not only as the "what is" of existence, but also how it works.

The word, theology, of course, comes from the Greek *Theos*, or God. *Logy* is Greek for discourse or study.

Today, theology does not refer to the study of Greek gods, nor the concepts held by those in an age when our knowledge of the cosmos was limited to a small section of the globe. To do theology today entails a multiverse of stars and life and mind for which there is no precedent in the past.

To do theology today is to make sense and meaning out of our life and time as near to the reality of our existence as we can observe and understand it.

But in today's space-time, where does one "stand under" to "observe" in this whereless world? Geographically, I'm a hundred miles north of the Arctic Circle in the wilderness of the Brooks Range in Alaska. I am somewhere. I could be anywhere at any time.

Sam Wright
Koviashuvik, Alaska

*The icy touch of space
reaches deep into
the Brooks Range in winter.*

January

I T IS EARLY MORNING on this first day of January. Moonlight reflects from snow crystals. They glitter through my cabin window, brightening the inside as much as noon-day is able at this time of winter dark.

The Fahrenheit thermometer on the spruce tree outside reflects the same forty degrees below zero that marked the turn of the year last night while northern lights swirled overhead. I listened to the traditional New Year celebrations throughout the world on my little radio.

As I listened, the earth turned from one time zone to another, from one year to the next.

When I lived in New Mexico I considered myself a resident of the far west until I moved a thousand miles farther west to dwell north of San Francisco on the edge of the Pacific Ocean. The state of Alaska reaches beyond the edge of west, farther west than Hawaii.

People think of Alaska in terms of north and south, but Alaska is so far west it projects across the international date line into tomorrow. I like being on the edge of tomorrow. The Eskimos have a word for this kind of place. It is Koviashuvik.

Weather

I have learned that I am a part of how weather is made.

From "up there" in outer space comes the cold which precipitates moisture from the air leaving arctic nights aglow with the Aurora Borealis and glistening stars.

The icy touch of space reaches deep into the Brooks Range in winter. Temperatures drop as many as sixty or seventy degrees below zero on the Fahrenheit thermometer outside our cabin window.

"Alapah!"—cold—becomes the Eskimo word of greeting. Weather is always in our conversation for weather dominates all life in the far north.

∾

The United States Weather Bureau in Fairbanks broadcasts a daily forecast over the radio. However, Koviashuvik is two hundred miles farther north and one hundred miles beyond the Arctic Circle. Forecasts for Fairbanks are often based upon what is moving inland from the Gulf of Alaska or the Bering Sea.

I am curious as to what makes weather here in the mountains of the Brooks Range. From here it usually moves east into Canada's Northwest Territories and often south into the northern United States.

First of all, I am aware that the weather is made by the sun. When daylight is continuous here in the summer, heat builds up as it is reflected from the earth. It can rise into the eighties and occasionally ninety in June. By November, when the sun is supplying light and heat for less than a couple of hours a day, the calories drain rapidly away. Temperatures soon average well below zero.

Far to the south of us, the Alaska Range of mountains helps seal the interior of Alaska from the warm moisture-bearing air of the Pacific Ocean. By the time the air gets over the Alaska Range, with its 20,320-foot Denali peak, it is relatively dry. The moisture having precipitated on its southern slopes.

Similarly, in a reverse way, the Brooks Range acts as a barrier to the arctic weather of the polar ice cap in the north. As a result, our southern slope of the Brooks Range has a dry sub-arctic climate much of the year.

However, in the winter, when a cold air mass starts building up north of the range, the cold spills over the mountains like water from behind a dam and flows across the Yukon Flats.

Temperatures along the Yukon River, to the south of our range, can drop to a recorded eighty degrees below zero. Then the white silence is broken only by dark patches of frozen forests of spruce trees. Nothing moves.

Here at Koviashuvik, on the southern slope of the Brooks Range, there is a normal pattern of steady lowering of temperatures during October. And when the sun disappears behind the mountains for the winter in November, temperatures average zero on the Fahrenheit scale.

Cold is relative. I have become aware that I also am part of the weather. As a rainbow is a relationship between sunlight, water particles, and the viewer, so do I participate in weather.

One morning in November, after building a fire in the Yukon Stove and putting coffee on to perk, I stepped outside, clothed in my normal waffle-weave underwear, khaki shirt, jeans, and boots.

For a moment I felt as if I were in the high Sierra Nevada of California in August, just before sunrise. If I had been asked how cold it was, I'd have said, "Frosty, maybe somewhere between 28 and 30 degrees."

Standing on the east side of our cabin, I had the feeling that if a glowing sun appeared over the mountains, its warmth would take the frost away except in places of shadow. Then, realizing where I was, and knowing that the sun would not appear over the mountains until February, and then only at mid-day, I was reminded that the two feet of snow was quite a "frost!"

I checked the thermometer in front of the cabin. It was seventeen degrees below zero.

I have felt colder at this time of year on the Mojave Desert. Although I could freeze to death more quickly here at seventeen below zero, I felt the cold much more intensely on the desert of the southwest in the lower forty-eight.

I have learned that my response to temperature includes many factors. First of all I am better prepared here for the cold, psychologically and physically, with caribou, moose, and bear fat as staples in my diet. Even so, there is some special quality about this northern cold which makes it an adventure instead of hardship. I know the dryness of the air helps, and I am careful not to expose fingers and ears too long.

As my neighbor, Erling Nesland, who trapped and panned gold about sixty miles from here at Tramway Bar, said, "In the Brooks along the Koyokuk there's no purgatory in winter. You're either alive or frozen to death."

Then, as if it were an afterthought, he said, "Denny O'Keef froze to death crossing the ice on your lake a while back. You can't be cold in winter, Sam. Warmth to numbness is no more than the edge of a skinning knife."

∽

January is the coldest month of the year. The maximum daily temperature averages well below zero. Even with this low average, temperatures as warm as freezing can occasionally occur when storm clouds blanket the range.

Snowfall is usually heavier in January than in any other month. An old-time miner told me of years when there was more than five feet of snow. Normally, however, the depth is seldom more than three feet.

∾

A few winters ago I awakened early on a January morning. Moonlight, reflecting on the snow, brightened both windows of the cabin as much as mid-day at this time of winter dark. I noted on the thermometer outside the window that it was fifty degrees below zero, the coldest it had been up to that time. Stepping outside in my lounging togs of insulated underwear, I found the weather relatively mild. If I had not had the thermometer for a guide, I would have estimated the cold at about twenty below. There seems to be no close relationship between thermometer temperatures and feeling temperatures in the lifestyle I have chosen here at this latitude.

Both food and fatigue affect the feeling of temperature. If I am particularly tired or hungry, I feel the cold much more. I am also aware of the fuel in caribou fat. The colder it is, the more my craving for fat increases. Not only do I understand the Eskimo diet in which fat is essential, but find myself choosing the fattiest piece of meat in the pot as the tastiest. Eskimo ice cream, which is a mixture of berries, sugar, and hot fat whipped into snow, would be unthinkable to me in the summer But in January I would not trade it for the choicest pie or tastiest custard.

Water still freezes or thaws when the thermometer registers thirty-two degrees, or zero on the centigrade scale. However, on the human scale, I have learned to say that "I" am cold, instead of "it" is cold. The "it" out there is only one piece of temperature in a much wider ecology we call weather.

January has taught me that there is also an "in here" thermometer, one that calculates much more than the glass tube with its rise and fall of mercury.

An Arctic Allegory
Of Him Who Would Trap a Wolverine

[*A note about parables and allegories:* Some of the oldest figurative forms of instruction are the allegory and parable. They were used not only by the oriental sages, early Greek scholars, and Rabbinical writers, but are also found in the tales and teachings of people the world round.

Allegories and parables from north of the Arctic Circle are gleaned from subsistence living in this last great wilderness. According to the *American College Dictionary*, an allegory is a story in which people, things, and happenings have another meaning, often morally instructive. A parable is a short allegorical story, designed to convey some truth or moral lesson.]

∾

Now on a certain day the man of Koviashuvik did go forth to see if a wolverine had been caught in his trap. Strapped he on his snowshoes after he had bundled up. With double felts in his mukluks he did cover his feet, inasmuch as the cold had dropped to forty below zero.

As beforetimes, the woman of wisdom said unto him: "Why goest thou into the wilderness during such cold when tomorrow may be warmer?"

And he answered her, saying: "Wantest thou to suffer the wolverine long in a steel trap? We should suffer it not, for of such comes the ruff for our parkas."

And so the man of Koviashuvik did mush forth, even into that far northern wilderness where few travel. And there did he approach the place wherein a wolverine trap had been set. And there did he see a movement in the snow.

Cocked he his rifle and cautiously approached. Only then did he see that the trap contained not a ferocious wolverine, but a small Alaska gray jaybird whose curiosity had cost its life.

Then thinketh the man of Koviashuvik with the clear wisdom that comes from the cold: "So it is among people. Not only can curiosity trap the unwary, but he who would catch a great prize may only get the bird."

Search for Koviashuvik

Kovi-a-shu-vik is an Eskimo word for living in the present moment with quiet joy and happiness. It is what Donna Lee and I call our wilderness home north of the Arctic Circle in the Brooks Range of Alaska.

Here is where, with my former spouse, Billie, I spent winters and summers in a twelve-by-twelve foot log cabin that I built with simple hand tools on a slope above a sparkling mountain lake. It is here in the isolation of this northern wilderness that Donna and I still return from our travels to gain perspective and relearn what it means to be fully at home and alive.

Koviashuvik is more than a geographic place, or a landscape in the mind, or the title of a book I wrote. It is about a way of seeing at a time when the myths by which we have lived in the past no longer support our hopes and dreams for the future.

As I wrote in *Koviashuvik*, In the past, old premises worked. The myths by which we lived seemed to confirm themselves. But now we are in a time of change and we question old patterns. No longer do we know if the universe is knowable, or if humans are rational. We do not know if there is everywhere a conformity to laws, or that the universe will provide for us, or if human life is sacred, or if freedom is real or good. We have lived by these myths but we could not see them as myths. Now we can.

So here we are at a time in our journey when the myths by which we have lived and the premises we have held may no longer fit. It is time to become explorers again in a new age rising all about us. It is a time for a renewed search.

In the search for Koviashuvik, I left my teaching role at the Starr King graduate seminary in Berkeley, California, in 1968 for the far north wildness of Alaska. It has since become my geographic home, where I continually return.

Billie died in 1987. The following summer, with her friend Donna Lee as my new spouse and adventuring companion, we scattered Billie's ashes as she had requested, on a knoll above our arctic lake, "where the cranberries grow reddest and finest."

Except for a few hand tools, a rifle, and staples, Billie and I lived off the land. Our winter meat was moose and caribou. We caught fish in the summer and picked berries in the autumn. We had a small radio receiver, but no way to call out. There were no roads, and the nearest pavement was 200 miles south. We flew in, landing on the lake in a small bush plane, with our few staples such as flour and sugar. We trapped and wrote for what little monetary income we needed, never enough to pay any income tax. What were we seeking? Why did we choose a home in this wilderness? Why do Donna and I still choose it today?

To speak of what I was seeking, I must go back a few years earlier when I left for the Mojave Desert in mid-summer and lived as our ancestors did with primitive tools fashioned from materials at hand. It was not the discipline of tenuous living I sought. I could always hike to my Jeep and drive out. It was a search for something I have observed in many people who live close to nature—that ancient realization of meaning and oneness so hard to know and recognize as life becomes increasingly involved. Where is it found in suburban living? How can it be a part of the modern life we are creating?

The cultural historian William Thompson has pointed out that dead ideas now support today's dying industrial civilizations, but new ideas hold the life of a whole culture for the earth. What these ideas call for is a re-visioning or a remythologizing of nature, self, and society.

The Wild

In this interconnected web of existence, the wild is a resource from which we can still gain sustenance for our spirit, know our roots, perhaps even save ourselves. As I look about us in our exploding urban world, it seems self-evident that we can no longer count on nature's world to reserve the wild for the future. It is up to us to preserve it within ourselves.

The human environment has many dimensions, not the least of which we create ourselves, from modern technology to a United Nations and from communities and parks to our art and poetry. The environment, whether inner or outer, is more and more our own creation. The ancient philosophical and religious questions "Who am I?" "Why am I here?" "Where am I going?" require new perspectives.

So I continue to return to this northern wilderness, convinced that answers to many questions raised by our crowded suburbs and tense world might be found here. In the search for

Koviashuvik I am here to live and learn what wilderness and its way of life might teach me that I might share with others.

The Eskimo

Some of what I am learning is from the Eskimo.

In the center of the Brooks Range, at Anaktuvuk Pass, lives a community of inland Eskimo, the Nunamiut, whose life is still tied to the migration of caribou.

A brief study made of these people in 1950 by a visiting Norwegian intrigued me. Here was a people for whom social and physical ecological factors seemed few and relatively clear. A community of about 120 people not yet smothered by modern society, whose way of life was bound to be changed soon by the pressures of our expanding western culture.

I hiked into the village on my first visit to Alaska in 1966 and became involved with the Ahgooks, the Paniaks, the Kakinyas, the Tobuks, and other families. I found individuals, not a category called "native" or "Eskimo." I ate their caribou, became ill, shared their jokes, and spoke in their religious service.

Two years later I returned to this Alaskan wilderness with Billie. We came to this remote area as part of my sabbatical year. I returned because here people were still living far from urban centers and I was interested in observing shifting value systems of cultures in rapid transition.

We remained in the wilderness on the shore of this isolated mountain lake, to live, to dig in, to learn. To learn about ourselves and human beings trying to survive in the new technological environment which we have created during the past few hundred years.

What did we learn? Much that cannot be put into simple phrases, but perhaps some of what we learned is in the telling of times, places, and environments in which we move and have our being.

An Eskimo Village

It was shortly before noon when I left the Ahgooks' snow-covered sod hut. The sun was still visible along the crest of the mountains which ringed the village. This was a time of transition before winter. In the summer this far north, night never arrives. In contrast, here, north of the Arctic Circle, the winters are long and dark. The sun will soon be gone.

Kakinya's sled dogs barked as they watched me snowshoe across the creek out of the mountain's shadow into sunlight. Then all was still except for the crunch of snow beneath my feet and the scrape of beard in the hood of my parka.

I was not the last visitor to leave the Ahgook dwelling, but I had recognized that the time for departure had come when an old man rose from the bundle of willow boughs, and without a word, left. The Nunamiut of the central Brooks Range do not comment with a good-bye on leaving.

We had just discussed how this had caused misunderstanding for Kanayuk, a young Eskimo who was living in a foster home in order to attend school away from the village.

"What native children need to be taught is manners," he had overheard from a telephone conversation. "We have had the boy as a guest in our home for nearly a week and he never so much as says, 'good-bye,' when he goes out."

This comment devastated Kanayuk. Without a word, he put his few possessions in a bag and left, hurt, still not saying "good-bye."

Authorities picked him up as a runaway and finally returned him to his village.

Now, several years later, sitting on the bundle of willows in his neighbor's sod hut, he said, "I was too dumb to learn to say good-bye. Too young I guess."

Jack Ahgook, who was leaning against the roof support pole said, "That's what we need, education. You can't do anything unless you go to school."

He paused as if the sentence were not finished, smiled and said, "Except hunt and shoot caribou."

Everybody laughed.

The old woman on the caribou skin across from me showed her few stubby yellow teeth as she laughed with the rest of us. She sat with both legs straight out in front of her and was sewing together a pair of skins from the legs of a caribou. She was making mukluks. Her craftsmanship was considered the finest in the village. I knew she was very old by her tattoos—which have not been done for many years. The three blue lines tattooed on her chin accented the wrinkles in her face. I doubt that she understood the conversation, but her laughter was spontaneous and genuine as she participated in the joke. She took stitch after stitch with fine caribou sinew, which she pushed through the skins with a sharp three-cornered needle. Her fingers were deft and rapid.

I nodded toward the old woman. "Did she learn to make such good mukluks from her mother?"

Lela Ahgook spoke to the old "grandmother" in Eskimo. The wrinkled face was very serious as she answered in the easy singsong of their dialect, ending with what was obviously a question.

When Lela responded, the old woman glanced at me with a look of wonder and then said something as if speaking to herself. Everyone broke into peals of laughter.

Lela tried to explain the laughter. When she repeated my question, something was lost in translation, and the old woman's answering question had been in effect, "Does Tannik (white man) want to do woman's work? Maybe he think he can have a baby?"

Then I joined the rest in hearty laughter.

༅

Outside the hut a sled dog howled. Another dog began to bark, and soon the barking and howling filled the mountain pass with its cacophony.

As I watched the old grandmother sewing the caribou skins, I was aware that this same scene and sounds had been present here long before Europeans dreamed of a continent beyond the sea.

For centuries, these people have camped in this mountain pass to await the caribou migration from the northern tundra as the herds streamed over the mountains toward the sheltered foothills of the southern Brooks Range; then, back to the arctic slope once more in the early spring. Like caribou, which the Nunamiut hunted, their lives were in balance with their environment.

༅

In September, Italook had returned from a scouting trip to the north, bringing news which was awaited by all in the village, "Caribou are coming!"

The scattered herds, which had spent the summer on the flat tundra between the mountains and the Arctic Ocean, were beginning to gather in the northern foothills. Any day now they would begin streaming through the passes to their wintering ground south of the range.

With the coming of caribou, life in the village quickly changed from the relaxed atmosphere of summer to expectant activity. Rifles were cleaned and ammunition checked. Sleds and dog harness were being repaired. Snowmachine engines were cranked up and sparkplugs replaced.

"Tuktu," caribou, could be heard frequently in nearly every conversation.

Even before Italook confirmed the movement of caribou, the village was aware of their approach. When I asked one of the hunters how he knew this, he said, "The ravens tell us. They have a different call. The old people say they call 'Tuktu! Tuktu!' when the caribou are coming."

There was no hunting of the first caribou which came through the pass. The vanguard of the migrating herds are not disturbed. "If you shoot the first caribou which appear, the others will turn back and tell the rest to go another way," an old hunter told me. He said, "Early days ago, a hunter killed the first caribou when they appeared and they went away. Many people were hungry and died that winter."

∽

This was my last visit among the people in the village at Anaktuvuk Pass—before the native land claims settlement and completion of the Trans-Alaska Pipeline Project changed their world forever. However, the inevitability of change had begun long before.

"We didn't need much money," Jack Ahgook told me when he was replacing a sparkplug in his snowmachine, "but now we are very poor."

He patted the seat of his snow machine, and with a chuckle said, "He don't eat caribou like dogs, but he sure like gasoline!"

∽

A way of life which had sustained the nomadic inland Eskimos of the Brooks Range began its drastic change with the grading of an airstrip on a gravel bar in Anaktuvuk Pass when Jack Ahgook was a child. Small groups of Nunamiut families, once scattered through the mountains, took up residence beside the airstrip. In 1960 this became a permanent village.

The Nunamiut chose settlement so they could utilize the seeming advantages of a rapidly advancing industrial society; particularly a school, a mission church, and the goods an airstrip would provide.

In 1963 the first snowmachine came into the village. By 1968 a majority of villagers had acquired them to replace sled dogs.

Jack put his tools into a battered lunch box and threw a caribou skin over the snowmachine.

"I sure wish I knew how to get some money," he said, as we walked toward his hut between empty gasoline cans and a snow-banked tent where his family lived during the summer. "I can't do anything because I don't have education. You can't make no money without lots of school."

As a result of the developing oil industry on the arctic slope of northern Alaska, a winter haul road was bulldozed over the Brooks Range, passing through Anaktuvuk Pass. When the road crew surveying the route reached the pass, they offered work to the village men to mark the road north with willow tripods every quarter mile for 170 miles, so drivers could find the route in drifting snows.

"It was pretty good," Jack told me. "I made about a thousan' dollars, I think."

When I asked what he did with his acquired wealth, he laughed, "Soon as us guys was paid we went to Fairbanks. Boy, we was broke when we come home!"

When sitting in his sod house, drinking tea with his neighbors, Jack spoke again of his thousand-dollar paycheck of last spring. He said it had cost him two hundred dollars in airfare to do his shopping in Fairbanks.

"I got lots of good things there, a tape recorder, a .243 rifle, and a bicycle. It was sure hard to ride that bike. Tulak has already broke it."

He leaned back against a bundle of caribou hides and reached into his pocket for a match to light his cigarette. He drew deeply and blew the smoke through pursed lips toward the top of the hut. "I got lots of stuff, some tricycles for the kids."

He looked at his wife sitting on a bundle of willow boughs. She was picking leaves and twigs out of a bowl of frozen blueberries.

"I got a washing machine too," he said. "It sure cost a lot. Cost four hundred and fifty dollars." He laughed and said, "Soon as the washing machine come the generator broke down. No clothes washed in it yet!"

"I put a caribou hide in to soak," Jack's wife said. "It pretty good for that."

This produced much laughter among the group in the hut.

I asked about hot water, as there was no plumbing in the village and they used melted snow or carried water in summer from the creek. Jack reached into a cardboard carton and held up a large soap box. Its colorful label stated that the content was cold water detergent.

"That cold water soap is pretty good for tanning caribou skin," Jack's wife said. "It much better than Tide. Tide make it yellow."

As always, the conversation returned to caribou.

"Maybe the caribou not come through Anaktukvuk no more when they make the road."

There was a long silence broken only by the sound of a dog barking in the distance.

"I'm going to build me a house as big as the school house," Jack said. "Then I could make money putting up them truck drivers."

Jack's wife stood up and put the bowl of blueberries on a shelf of the open cupboard made of stacked wooden fuel can boxes. "I think maybe it will be different here when we have truckers all the time," she said.

After following Kanayuk from the hut and crossing the creek, I snowshoed up the mountain slope above the scattering of sod huts, tents, and dwellings recently constructed of plywood, which the Bureau of Indian Affairs had flown in for the villagers.

In 1967 there was an attempt to move the village to a new site because the willows burned for fuel were nearly depleted. The villagers voted not to move, even through the hardship was obvious.

"One time I left Anaktuvuk to work in Fairbanks," Noah Ahgook told me, "but I come back pretty fast when they give me my money. I don't think I go away again no more, I think I stay here."

The tops of oil drums stacked beside the snow-covered gravel airstrip reflected the slanting sunlight like mirrors. To the north, the blue-white mountains lifted above the pass which stretched to the arctic slope where thousands of caribou spend the summer.

This place of beauty had been a traditional campsite for the inland Eskimo. Here they gathered each year by Raven Lake to meet the migrating caribou. Here, families were reunited. Here, young people met and new families began. I could see several wooden crosses, standing black against the snow-covered tundra west of the lake. I could understand the deep ties to this place.

However, there is a change in the children. Last autumn the schoolteacher asked the twenty-one children between grades four and eight, "Where would you like to live in the future?"

Fifteen said Fairbanks; four Anchorage; one outside Alaska; and one undecided. No one said he or she would live in Anaktuvuk Pass.

As the sun dipped below the mountain skyline, a wolf howled in the distance. Then the mountains swallowed the sound.

This was my last visit with friends in Anaktuvuk Pass. I've since learned that snowmachines have now replaced sled dogs and hunters have to travel many miles to find caribou. I also learned that Jack Ahgook, along with other friends returning from Fairbanks, was killed when his plane crashed on the airstrip in a snow squall. I may never return. I want to remember Anaktuvuk as it was.

Worth-Shape

In an infinite calculus
Time and all patterns,
Things, people, and thoughts,
Are divisions of space.

Worth-shape is a whole, not a part,
Yet than being, becoming is more.

Hunt, in laughter and tears,
For a cause that creates and sustains and destroys;
In tension find truth:
And look for beginnings in ends.

A Polar Parable
Of Rotting Ice

On a certain day it came to pass that the man of Koviashuvik went forth on the ice to chop a hole wherein he might fish for the great trout which swam beneath him. The winter had been exceeding long and meat in the cache had dwindled.

From the hole he made in the ice, he brought forth a great fish. Howsoever, the ice did tremble and he was sore afraid.

In the cabin, the woman of wisdom took delight in the great fish which the man of Koviashuvik had brought forth. Even so, she did speak her concern that the ice trembled, and did inquire: "How thick is the ice that remaineth?"

The man of Koviashuvik answered her, saying: "Two, peradventure three feet."

Then the woman of wisdom sayeth: "With such thick ice thou art surely safe."

Whereupon the man of Koviashuvik replied: "Nay, it is not so. Although the ice appears thick as ever, underneath it has candled and eroded in the rising warmth. It can break asunder beneath my feet without warning. I can trust it no more."

Then thinketh he: "So it is throughout the world wherein much seemed to have the strength of old, albeit that which gave support in the past can no longer be trusted."

Postscript

They had what the world has lost [Native Americans], they have it now. What the world has lost, the world must have again, lest it die. This is not merely a passing reference to World War III or to the atomic bomb, although the reference includes these ways of death too. They had this power for living which our modern world has lost, as world-view and self-view, as tradition and institution, as practical philosophy dominating their societies and as an art supreme among all the arts. They were at one with their gods.

—John Collier, former United States Commissioner of Indian Affairs

On Ground Hog Day I saw
my shadow for the first time
since November.

February

I SAW MY SHADOW for the first time since November on this second day of February. In the tradition of the Eskimo, I threw back the ruff from my head and raised my arms to greet Sikrinik at this first appearance of the golden sun after seventy-seven days.

In the early Christian calendar, the second day of February was known as Candlemas, or the blessing of candles. In New England, it is called Ground Hog Day. But north of the Arctic Circle there is no woodchuck coming out to see its shadow—not at this latitude.

Seeing my shadow is a new experience after the long winter dark. Much that seemed hidden is revealed. I am seeing what I knew before, but seeing in a new way.

I can see more clearly now the shadow of denigration of the individual. What tended to be hidden in the urban society that I left now stands out in sharp contrast: Persons carried into darkness with a sense of helplessness by vast, inhuman forces which seemed elusive and inexorable. In that darkness people were depersonalized, demoted into things. The ancient dualisms of quantity and quality, of technology and personality, of dark and light, still play their ancient roles.

As the shifting earth exposes the sun, showing our shadows, we can better view ourselves in our unique humanness without continuing on the self-destructive path we so lemming-like appear to be following.

"Sikrinaktok!": The sun shines!

Weather

By February, the thermometer usually begins a slow upward trend. However, according to record, this month has at times been the coldest of the year. Precipitation in February is much less than in January.

Looking back in my journal, I note that according to the radio news from Fairbanks, our cold had drifted south to there. All schools except the University of Alaska were temporarily closed due to the cold weather. Fairbanks had registered sixty degrees below zero.

The cold our unofficial thermometer registered here was seventy-six degrees below zero.

An Arctic Allegory
Of Being Up a Tree

It came to pass in the year of the deep snow that Aklak, the great grizzly bear, failed to hibernate. Neither cave nor shelter did he find before the freezing winds swept down the mountains from the arctic sea. Tramped he miles in search of the wolf's kill. Dug he fruitlessly in the snow for low bush cranberries which remain fresh-frozen all winter. In his hair did ice collect. Moreover, the frost of winter built up around his eyes and his vision was much encumbered.

Thus, did the great bear fail to see the man of Koviashuvik. Nor did the man of Koviashuvik see the great bear lumbering toward him as he pisseth in the snow.

And so, did Aklak approach the man of Koviashuvik, who expected not a bear in winter.

The man of Koviashuvik tarried not but did scramble up a small spruce tree unrelieved, even with his snowshoes still attached!

However, the bear knew not the man didst climb a tree for frost had dimmed his vision. He passed on.

Then pondered the man of Koviashuvik while hanging in the tree: "So it is among those who find no shelter from the cold. Their eyes are dimmed. As ice collects in their souls they starve in their hearts. Even so, they put another who is going about his business up a tree."

Odyssey and the Meaning of Covenant

Stories of life journeys are often called odysseys from Odysseus's wandering journeys in Greek mythology.

This particular experience is from my own life odyssey here at Koviashuvik. It is one that has occurred and continues to occur in varying and differing ways in all of our lives. We are ever poised on the edge where we can look into darkness in many forms, from cancer and AIDS to those intangible unknowns we all share that are often difficult to articulate.

Here, deep in this winter season, culminating in a spring celebration of rebirth and renewal, seems an appropriate time to explore experiences of those darker times of our lives. If they are to be illuminated and transcended, they call upon our own human awareness and courage to reach toward a renewal of spirit and hope.

The metaphor I use is personal. The place, here at Koviashuvik, my home where Billie and I lived alone for many years. Where—despite the sixty to seventy degrees below zero winters, and the isolation, and absence of so-called comforts of civilization—we found unbelievable joy and beauty and peace. For us then, and for me now, this is a sacred place.

Some time ago, this sacred place of Koviashuvik was violated, and thereby I felt violated and so did Billie. I want to tell about it because it symbolizes for me the inevitable hardship we encounter when we dare to try to live our lives as sacred journeys, even as we know these are always journeys of risk.

∾

Billie and I had been working with our Unitarian Universalist wilderness group at a retreat center in the mountains of central Arizona. We came home to Koviashuvik with a sense of joy (as always) of expectation, of curiosity about whether the exquisitely beautiful arctic terns, who fly 11,000 miles from Tierra Del Fuego to nest here at our...and their...arctic lake, were still here, or had left for their return flight with their young.

Or, whether the fine, fat char (lake trout) would soon be spawning off the point of Nukuchluk's grave...where Billie's ashes are now scattered among the scarlet lingonberries.

As our small amphibian bush plane sat down on the sparkling, azure waters of our lake, the bush pilot revved the engine, let down its wheels, and the little plane waddled awkwardly up onto the spit of land across the bay from our cabin.

While the pilot and Billie unloaded supplies, I hiked over to our cabin to get the small aluminum river boat which had been flown in at great expense a few years before and was stored in a log shed attached to our dwelling. The boat was gone.

We scanned the shoreline, wondering if some fisherman from a passing float plane had perhaps borrowed it and failed to return it or failed to berth it securely on the shore. But it was not in sight.

We packed supplies over to the cabin. Someone had obviously used it in our absence. But then we always leave our doors unlocked and open to anyone who may need shelter or food. In the past, a few such wanderers had made use of our home. We have had fliers weathering in, waiting out a storm in our little log cabin, and hikers, weary of fighting mosquitoes or keeping an alert for grizzlies while camping out of doors.

When food supplies had been used from the cache, the borrowers had always replaced them, shipping them in by the next mail plane. Or they had left money and a thank you note on our table. No one had ever taken advantage of, or abused, our hospitality and home.

There is a code of the far north which still prevails. In religious terms we would call it a "covenant." It is a code evolved out of the dictates of a particular environment, and it demands that we care for each other. It does not say that we have to like each other; it says only that we must care for each other. Our individual survival in the arctic is marginal and we must honor our collective survival. It is the same covenant we all share with the Chinese, the Russians, the Muslims, with each other...a code for the survival of our species and of the earth.

As I went out to chop wood to start a fire in the Yukon Stove, I found that all our axes were gone. When Billie went up into the cache to get the food supplies we had left, she found it empty. Our fishing poles and gear were gone. Our basic hand tools were gone, as was our snowmobile brought in at considerable cost by the small ski plane flying over 200 miles from Fairbanks. And its toboggan on which we hauled our winter wood.

Checking further, now stunned with disbelief, we found all our snowshoes missing. Our winter survival clothing—mitts, parkas, thermal underwear, wool trousers, arctic boots. All our mukluk fur boots, crafted for us by Eskimo friends at Anaktuvuk Pass were gone.

We had been left helpless to survive, without even an axe or saw to get wood for our cooking and heating. Had we come home in the winter, as we had planned, we would have arrived, trusting that we had all the basic necessities for survival. We would have found no snowshoes, no arctic clothing, no axes, no transport, no food.

Whoever had done this thing was essentially a potential murderer, for our survival, under such circumstances, was very much in jeopardy.

Calculating the length of time we could now get along on the limited supplies we had just brought in, and borrowing an axe from the survival gear kept in all far northern bush planes, we set a new, much closer time to be picked up and checked the date with our pilot. We said good-bye and watched him take off to circle the lake, searching for any sign of our boat.

He soon buzzed the cabin and waggled his wings: This was the pre-arranged signal that there had been no sign of the boat. He then rose steeply over the mountains to the south to return to Fairbanks.

〜

Early the next morning, with a few days' supplies and my rifle, I took off. We were quite sure we knew who the thief was. We were not sure that we had ever met him but we had heard over the arctic grapevine about this young man who had, a year or two before, come into the country from parts unknown. He had made the wilderness residents uneasy with his disregard for others, his curiosity about the location of cabins—especially those with their owners away, and with his outlander's questions of where the most profitable mining claims were located. We thought he might be working someone else's claims some miles from us over the mountains. I meant to find him and our missing things.

I spent days hiking through the rough country looking for the thief. I talked with miners, flown in for the summer, with their dream of finding a little more gold in the creek...miners whose equipment and food cached over the winter had also been stolen by the same thief. They offered to join the search up another canyon where they knew of a trapper whose cache and equipment had also been pilfered.

We continued our searches across the high crags and deep hidden ravines of the range. But neither thief nor the missing materials were to be found.

∾

Squatting by my fire after the fourth day, I realized that my spirit had not been renewed by my return to Koviashuvik. More than this, I was filled with frustration and rage and ultimately helplessness. And when I returned to the cabin I found Billie feeling the same.

Suddenly, like never before at Koviashuvik, we could not see the arctic terns swooping gracefully in their lightning-quick dives for the small fish in the shallows, or hear the scolding cries of the parent loons as they urged their fledglings into practicing long runs across the lake waters in order to become airborne.

The small wild cranberries crimsoning on the tundra were only so many wild berries, not the rich harvest Billie had collected so gleefully each year in the past. The shortening days of early autumn with their constant play of shifting light and sun and clouds passed by without the joyous attention we usually gave them.

We were fixed, caught in a kind of no exit in our life journey. I, who by profession was called a "peace-maker," was obsessed with fury, anger, frustration, and pain at the defilement of this sacred place, at what seemed to me to be this violation of my very being.

My journeying, the adventure of my life, had gone awry. I was at an impasse, with no clear signal of how to proceed, of how to move on.

∾

We all know these psychological, these spiritual cul de sacs. These places where the path seems unexpectedly to end, and there is no clear way to continue on. We all know these moments of the journey where the journey seems to stop cold, where no map exists and no signals beckon us forward.

When we are there, immobilized by the harsh and painful realities our lives encounter, how do we find our way out? How do we let go of despair so that our lives move on, our journeying resumes? How do we once again come to see the glass as half-full rather than half-empty? How and from where do we summon up what Ed Abbey called our antidotes to despair?

Billie and I seriously talked about lighting a match to our cabin as we left, with the possibility of never returning.

∾

Caught in this trap of despair, what insights, what experiences, what wisdom could be called upon to serve as those antidotes?

I was overwhelmed with feelings of rage, with no way to express it except in the fantasy that should this thief appear in my gun-sight, I would not hesitate to treat him like any other rogue animal whose actions threatened my life. And this fantasy, I also knew, was not so unlikely, as I have a longtime familiarity with a rifle as well as other tools.

But that I should be put into a situation where I could imagine using such a weapon against another human being, outside of an immediate life and death confrontation, only added to my rage and sense of helplessness.

As we all must in times of soul crisis (and I felt I was in such a crisis), I needed to find some way to regain my objectivity, my perspective. I tried to think of sources of help from my past. Help from other experiences which might hold insights to deal with this event.

One was the world of nature where the sacredness of the wild had given me perspective when the turmoil of urban life became too much. But it was the very desecration of this quality that had me trapped.

I probed my memory for words of wisdom from the great companions of the books I have shared. From Alfred North Whitehead, Gregory Bateson, Paul Tillich, Joseph Campbell, the poets, the philosophers, Ecclesiastes, the Way of the Tao, and on and on. I listened for the echo so often returned from these wisdom sources. But if there were echoes, this time they were too faint for me to hear.

I remembered how Billie's fear of our local grizzly bears had suddenly vanished after the third time the same bear had destroyed our cabin home and everything in it. How she kept her 30.06 rifle ready by the door when I was away, hoping, and as she said, "praying that this grizzly would return," so she could put an end to him and his destructiveness. A trade off, of sorts: Anger taking the place of fear. But what was to take the place of my present anger?

I recalled a friend of mine who lost the use of his legs in a mountain climbing accident when I was a graduate student at the University of New Mexico in Albuquerque, and whose life view through the whole tortuous experience was dominated by his cold, steely anger. Anger at his circumstances, at his religion, his God. And how I intuitively knew—that contrary to the nurses, doctors, and chaplain's prescription that he be encouraged to give up his anger—I must honor his rage, for it was that rage which gave him the strength, the will to endure. Later was time for grieving, and perhaps acceptance.

In sharing his trials, I learned that behind so much of our suffering is a sense of loss. For Frank, the loss of his legs, his freedom, his independence, the loss of a part of himself, a part of his life, a part of his identity.

And whether it be a loss of a friend, through misunderstanding or an action which violates our own moral sense, a loss of a long-familiar intimate through divorce, or a loved one through death, the loss of a job, a needed income, a valued belief, an image of self, trust in another, trust in the universe, trust in a just world, a fall from innocence. Whatever the loss, we suffer, we grieve.

∽

As time passed after my search for this man who had so casually, so unthinkingly violated our lives, the rage I felt slowly dissipated. The sense of disbelief numbed, and all that was left of feeling was an amorphous, non-focused sense of loss. Loss because of an act that, despite its consequences, was essentially meaningless. And thus, leaving behind a larger meaninglessness, a sense that nothing was inviolate, nothing was sacred. Our universe of beauty and goodness and harmony that was Koviashuvik, was, through this violation of me and my spirit, meaningless.

◠

When that feeling of alienation occurs, we are cut off from life; we are withdrawn from life. We are no longer in the world.

As Sheldon Kopp has written: The civility which separates us from the other animals depends upon the making and keeping of promises, vows, covenants. We are the only species to covenant with each other.

To me, covenant is sacred trust. I knew that our covenant of the far north, which carries within it the best of the covenants we may make with one another, had been betrayed. And because of this betrayal, this loss, I was entrapped. My spirit was caged, no longer free for journeying, for being "in" the world.

◠

We left Koviashuvik when the bush plane came in to get us and reported the event to the troopers in Fairbanks before heading back "outside" to Arizona.

◠

I use the word faith sparingly, for faith, like spirit, means too many different things to too many people to ever be certain of what we are really talking about. However, I can and do use the word faith to describe my assurance that, caught within that trap where journeying seems to cease, if we have patience to await the right moment of wisdom, the meaningful signal, and if we have the courage to allow ourselves to blindly move on, unseeing and uncertain through the darkness of despair toward the light of healing and renewed meaning, the way ahead will be revealed.

All of our entrapments, all our blind alleys have their exits. They are revealed to us only when we are ready to move on, to leave behind entrapment, betrayal, loss. But just when or how this moment comes remains a mystery for me, a mystery I have come to accept as I have observed it in wild animals which seem so quickly to put their betrayals and tragedies behind them.

For me there is no predictable moment, no premonition of a signal for how or when the door shall be opened to us. All I know for certain is that I have faith that it will be opened. It is this curious faith in life itself, in our endurance, our necessity for experiencing life in the world with all its tragedy, its joy, its blessings, its pain, which most sustains us through its inevitable times of despair and meaninglessness.

∽

Frozen into that cul de sac of the event experienced here at Koviashuvik, I longed for a door to open, to reveal to me once more the magic, the necessity of journeying in the world so abundant all around. And my longing was eventually answered, although I'm still not quite sure exactly when.

Perhaps it was on our return to the wilderness retreat in the beautiful wild Arizona mountains of the Sierra Anchas, sacred ancestral home of the Anasazi Indians. Perhaps it was there that something began to call, to invite me to share its wonders, to taste its delights, to share its mysteries, to journey once again through its sacred landscapes. Or perhaps it was the moment when an enchanting microcosm of aliveness in the form of a tiny hummingbird appeared soon after I refilled its feeder. Or was it a neighbor's baby's smile, which suddenly shone through to me like a flower opening to the morning sun? Or was it when I could again observe and feel, as if for the first time, the love of my closest companion, my spouse, and her support and understanding? Or when I could observe and really feel, as if for the first time, her sense of loss?

Or was it that I was simply bored with anger and grieving? Or was it something beyond, something transcendent of any of these?

And so time passed, time enough for transformation. For at some point in time, without my even realizing it, my journey seemed to have resumed itself, to have begun again, one moment at a time, one step at a time. I could begin to see clearly much unfinished and very interesting business of living awaiting my attention.

And with the cool, free air of renewed journeying now flowing through the open door of my imagined impasse came quiet, welcomed moments of reflection—of understanding. For the unexamined life, the life lived without profound reflection and effort at understanding its meaning, is life lived merely on the surface of things. It is life lived on the most trivialized plane of existence.

And what of Koviashuvik? Was it changed by this event? Or was it I who was changed? Was I made more vulnerable by this experience? Or was I strengthened? Was I left mistrustful of covenant? Or more trustful because this event proved once again how necessary, how meaningful it is when we are able to honor our covenant with one another? Did I come to appreciate Koviashuvik less because pain and despair had entered into this earthly Eden of mine?

No. It is still here, timeless, beautiful beyond imagination, now white and pristine with the snows of winter and covered with stillness but for the wild free songs of the wolves and the soft drowsy murmurs of the great grizzlies as they lie in their hidden places of winter's hibernation.

Awe and mystery still reside here among the sky-reaching mountain peaks. The sweet cold air from the north promises the certainties of more winters to come, followed inexorably by the certainties of springs to come when thousands of migrating birds will once again arrive. The clamor of their joyous songs will fill the air until the quietness of summers to come will fill nests with the future—a future which will need care and attention if downy chicks are to survive and grow to their own time of journeying.

Yes, Koviashuvik is still here, still a sacred place, just one of so many on this beautiful, most sacred place of all, the earth, our home.

Doxology

Though earth sings in the throats of birds,
Is lyric in the flashing sea
In us alone it wills and dreams,
Through us it sings of things to be.

A Polar Parable
Of Trails

On a certain day the man of Koviashuvik did hike into the wilderness to see what he could see even as the bear that went over the mountain.

And it came to pass that a blizzard did sweep from the sky and wind blew the snow into great drifts. The ground and sky seemed one. Also, a white-out did make it impossible to see whence he came. Then the man of Koviashuvik became confused, knowing not the west from the east or the north from the south.

And then on a tree did he find a blaze, which in early days ago had been cut there by men of old. And he did rejoice that he had a trail to follow. Howsoever, he saw that the blazes were twain, and did separate into two trails. Therewith the man of Koviashuvik did choose one even as all must.

From blaze to blaze did he hike until he caught himself standing at the edge of an abyss. And there he nearly stepped from the high bluff to the frozen creek below. Peradventure, the spring torrent after break-up had cut the trail asunder and he had paused just in time to save himself.

Then the man of Koviashuvik returned to where he began. And there he found the blazes of the other trail which led to his cabin.

Pondering the ways of trails and men, he said to himself: "How often are there two trails to follow. And like unto these, one leadeth to a warm fire while the other leadeth to destruction, albeit both are blazed all the way."

Postscript

The death of religion comes with the repression of the high hope of adventure.
—Alfred North Whitehead

A snug cabin.

March

FLYING NORTH ACROSS the snow-covered Yukon River through a grey-white sky, there is little evidence that this is the first day of spring. From now on days will become longer than nights until dimming stars are replaced by the midnight sun.

In this bush plane, the air is heavy with six sled dogs panting and restless in their chains. The Eskimo boy from Anaktuvuk Pass is also restless as he watches them stand and turn, seeking a more comfortable place to lie down. Both boy and dogs seem impatient to be back in their familiar snowbound village after hectic days of dogsled racing in Fairbanks.

I too am impatient to return to our northern mountain wilderness after a week of meetings, appointments, telephoning, and supermarkets.

I enjoyed visiting town after six months isolation in the snow-locked fastness of the mountains. Now it is good to be flying back home.

The Eskimo boy turns to me and smiles. He points to the cabin window, then shifts his position and tightens his seatbelt.

As the jagged peaks of the Brooks Range loom ahead, I return his smile and give my own seatbelt a tug.

It will be another two months before break-up, but now the caribou are starting their migration north over the snow-covered mountains. The boy and I share a secret with them.

We know deep in our bones that spring has arrived!

Weather

March is even drier than February. With the days as long as the nights, near the end of the month the minimum temperature is usually above zero. Blowing winds are uncommon on the south slope of the range, but in the past March has produced a few blows from the southeast with gusts up to fifty miles an hour.

Wind is that part of the weather which interests the inland Eskimos the most. In the major valleys of the Brooks Range the wind usually blows up or down the drainages. Unlike the southern slope, winds can blow from any direction on the north slope. In spring, wind can sweep across the frozen tundra north of the range without let-up from three to four weeks at a time.

Although a sense of direction when traveling in these roadless mountains is maintained primarily from the terrain, the Nunamiut are particularly aware of the direction of the wind.

White-outs, or heavy fog, frequently blanket the mountains so that it is impossible to see more than a few feet ahead. When features of the land are not visible, wind is the primary guide for maintaining a sense of direction. Not only can the pattern of a slight breeze be felt with face, hands, or body, but snow drifts make it possible to keep a constant check on any change in the wind's direction.

Late one day, when hunting for our winter meat, I was caught by darkness before I had finished skinning a caribou. Snowshoeing back to the cabin, I had to cross several miles of frozen lake. By the time I reached the plain of snow-covered ice, fog had settled so thickly that it was impossible to see any landmark. Although I could not see beyond the front bow of my snowshoes, using the slight drift of wind as a guide I was able to cover the miles to our cabin without mishap.

Perhaps wind is also a guide for caribou, who, stimulated by the rising temperatures and lengthening days in March, begin their migration north across the mountains.

An Arctic Allegory
Of Eating They Know Not What

Now it came to pass that the days were lean in the year of the great snow. The ribs of the sled dogs showed like frames of spruce-pole beds because caribou migrated not from the valley of the Yukon and meat was scarce in the land.

Then thinketh the man of Koviashuvik as he skinned the fox he had caught in his trap: "Even so, this flesh is red meat. Of it a stew I shall make for the dogs with the adding of bacon fat. The dogs shall know it as a savory dish from the table. Peradventure they shall wax strong."

Not only the flesh of the fox did he make into a savory dish, but the lynx of the forest also. Even so, the great wolf who giveth up his fur to the trapline did he also save for stew. And the sled dogs did wax fat. And frozen stew was plentiful in the cache as winter passed unto spring.

Then it came to pass that on a certain day men of affairs, who see that fish and game are taken within the law, did come in their ski-plane even as on wings of an eagle. And the man of Koviashuvik did snowshoe down the mountain and onto the frozen lake to greet them and invite them to partake of the bounty of his home.

In the cabin the woman of wisdom did scurry about to make repast, saying: "Known I that they were coming, with sourdough would I a cake have baked."

When all arrived in the cabin, there was much palaver. And great was the repast set before those who protect the fish and game.

After more palaver, these men of affairs did again mount up like eagles to return to the great city from whence they came.

Then sayeth the man of Koviashuvik to the woman of wisdom: "Great art thou among women who preparest a table before guests full to overflowing. Yea, with an empty pot didst thou bring forth plenty, even as the loaves and fishes of old."

The woman of wisdom said: "Nay, praise me not. It is thee who deserveth the honor for thy frugality in reserving stew for such a time. Thou art a clever rascal to keep a reserve in the cache."

Then gazed they at each other. And they did grow pale in their faces knowing that it was for the dogs.

Then the man of Koviashuvik made a wan smile and said: "So it is among people as among dogs. They shall partake of they know not what and still wax strong."

Wild Facts and Koviashuktok

As sunlight glitters through our cabin window this still morning in March, I am reminded that it was at this early time of year that Donna and I were jammed in an old forty passenger school bus with one hundred Guatemalans for eight hours.

We lurched, slid, and ground through mud holes on a new road cut through the wild rainforest of Guatemala. This new road began near the border of southern Mexico from where, with our backpacks, we were on our way to the Mayan jungle ruins of Tikal in the Peten. The Peten, the wild rainforest of Guatemala, has been called a lung of the earth, one of its great oxygen producers.

∾

I am aware, on this sparkling March morning, that if today is a typical day on this planet earth we will lose one hundred and sixteen square miles of rainforest. That is about one acre a second.

I am also aware that at the same time we will lose another seventy square miles to encroaching deserts as a result of human management—or mismanagement—and overpopulation. We will lose forty to one hundred species, and no one knows whether the number is forty or one hundred, or more or less.

The day you read this, the human population will increase by more than 250,000. This is more than half the population of the state of Alaska. We will also add 2,700 tons of chlorofluorocarbons to the atmosphere, as well as 15,000,000 tons of carbon. Tonight, the world will be a little hotter and its waters more acidic. The world's population will rise by more than 90,000,000 people this year. And by the year 2000, the best conservative calculations predict that as many as 20 percent of the life forms that were here on earth in the year 1900 will be extinct. I find these numbers staggering.

Many things on which our future health and prosperity depend are in dire jeopardy. And though we have heard this over and over, not many of us recognize and accept it.

The facts are that climate stability, the resiliency and productivity of natural systems, biological diversity, and even the beauty of the natural world are in such jeopardy that meaningful recovery is questionable. The truth is, we humans are in real trouble.

Worst of all, this is not the work of ignorant, uneducated people. I know this to be the case here in Alaska. Those who have brought this about are people with bachelor's degrees, master's degrees, law degrees, and doctorates. Obviously something was wrong with their education. And what was wrong, and still is, is that it emphasized theories instead of values, concepts rather than human beings, abstractions rather than consciousness, answers instead of questions, ideology and efficiency rather than conscience. The point is that knowledge, as we generally think of it, is no guarantee of decency or wisdom.

As I sit in my snug cabin in this northern wilderness, I am not arguing for ignorance. Rather that knowledge must be measured against standards of decency, care, and human survival. These are the economic, social, and religious issues we face as we look toward the twenty-first century, not only here in Alaska, but everywhere. What went wrong? In philosophical, spiritual, or religious terms, what went wrong is spelled out in *Moby Dick* by Herman Melville's Captain Ahab who says "All my means are sane, my motive and object mad." Or by a Dr. Frankenstein who refuses to take responsibility for his creation.

Today we are aware of the dominance of the analytical mind over that part given to creativity, humor, and wholeness.

Anyway, my theme is that this separation of self and object has laid a foundation for modern knowledge which has become our mythic tradition. Tragically, it is accepted without question. Unless we recognize the myth and the many other myths that flow from it, a viable future seems doomed.

～

David Orr, in a commencement address several years ago, spoke of five of these unquestioned myths. There are many more. However, on this sparkling March day these five seem particularly relevant.

The first is that ignorance is a solvable problem. Actually it is an inescapable part of the human condition. Like a light in the darkness, as it shines brighter, the circle of darkness beyond is proportional. The advance of knowledge always carries with it the advance of some form of ignorance. For example: In 1930 when Thomas Midgely, Jr. discovered chlorofluorocarbons, we were ignorant of stratospheric ozone and climatic stability. Today that ignorance has become a critical, life-threatening gap in the human understanding of the biosphere.

It wasn't until the 1970s that a few people began to ask, "what does this substance do to what?" In 1986 we discovered that chlorofluorocarbons had created a hole in the ozone over the South Pole the size of the lower forty-eight states, and by now a serious general thinning of ozone is worldwide. About the only place its meaning begins to touch us today is when dermatologists harp about skin cancer and its statistical increase. With the discovery of chlorofluorocarbons knowledge increased, but like the circumference of an expanding circle, ignorance grew as well.

A second myth is that with enough technology and knowledge we can—and I quote from *Scientific American*—"manage planet earth." This has a nice ring to it, especially where we've been managing plant and animal production. Also, it appeals to our fascination with digital readouts and computers. But any ecologist who is not trapped in the myth will tell you that the ecology of one square inch of topsoil is still largely unknown, and its relationships to the larger system of the biosphere point to complexities of earth and life systems that could probably never be safely managed.

What might be managed is human desire. But our attraction is caught by those things that avoid hard choices implied in our politics, morality, ethics, and common sense. We might think of ourselves fitting into an ecology more than the attempt to reshape the planet to fit our infinite wants.

A third myth is that knowledge is increasing. There certainly is a data explosion going on—words, digits, and paper. But this explosion should not be mistaken for an increase in knowledge, which cannot be so easily measured. While some knowledge is increasing, other kinds of knowledge are being lost.

There is a realization that something strange, if not dangerous is afoot as we lose personal contact with the earth. Year by year the number of people with first-hand experiences in the land dwindles as rural populations continue to shift to cities. In the wake of this loss of personal and local knowledge—the knowledge from which a real geography is derived, the knowledge on which a country must ultimately stand—has come something hard to define, something sinister and unsettling.

In the confusion of data with knowledge is a deeper concern, that learning will make us better people. But learning is endless and in itself will never make us ethical. Ultimately, it may be the knowledge of the good that is most threatened by all of our other advances.

All things considered, it is possible that we are becoming more ignorant of the things we must know to live well and sustainably on the earth.

A fourth myth is that we can adequately restore that which we have dismantled. The myth is obvious if we consider the physical world, such as the Hetch Hetchy and Owens Valley in California, or the long-term results of the Trans-Alaska Pipeline and the Valdez oil spill. But much more sinister is the way we have fragmented everything into bits and pieces called disciplines and subdisciplines, sealed from other such disciplines. As a result, after sixteen or even twenty years of so-called education, most students graduate without any broad, integrated sense of the unity of things or the consequences for their personhood, or the planet at large.

For example, we routinely produce economists who lack the most rudimentary knowledge of ecology. This might explain why our national accounting systems do not subtract the costs of biotic impoverishment, soil erosion, poisons in the air and water, and resource depletion when calculating the gross national product. We add the price of the sale of a bushel of wheat to the GNP while forgetting to subtract the three bushels of topsoil and other factors lost in its production. As a result we have fooled ourselves into thinking we are much richer than we are.

And a fifth myth is that our culture with its modern technology somehow represents a pinnacle of human achievement. Actually it represents cultural arrogance of the worst sort. It is a gross misreading of history and anthropology. One form of this view is that we won the Cold War with the triumph of capitalism over communism. Communism failed because it produced too little at too high a cost. However, capitalism is also failing because it produces too much and shares too little, also at too high a cost to our children and their children and grandchildren.

As an ascetic morality, communism failed, but so will capitalism because it destroys morality altogether. We have built a world of wealth for a few and poverty for a growing underclass. The fact is that at the moment we are living in a disintegrating culture. I say this because it does not nourish that which is best or noblest in the human spirit. It does not cultivate vision, imagination, or aesthetic or spiritual sensitivity. Nor does it encourage gentleness, generosity, caring, or compassion. Increasingly, as we end the twentieth century, the economic-technocratic-statist world view has become a destroyer of what is loving and life-affirming. We can see this looking at an oil rich Saddam Hussein in Iraq but not at ourselves.

∽

OK, Sam, here we are over the fiery pit, north of the Arctic Circle in March. How do we turn around? Do you have any positive suggestions to offer?

Yes, I think the first step, the very first step toward redirection, must be a widespread recognition that something is wrong, that present policies do not work, that what I call wild facts must be taken seriously. Unfortunately, the first step has not been taken by the public at large or their political leaders. Most politicians either do not understand that the situation has changed or fear to address the issue publicly. The press occasionally reports the wild facts, but then goes back to its usual news as if nothing has happened.

Besides recognizing that something is wrong, a second step is our need to recognize that the problems we face today are interconnected and thus have a common source. The recognition of this ecology in itself would help relieve the sense of generalized distress that many feel, or resist. A sense of being overwhelmed by unnamable powers might be overcome with its causes identified and named. Then human responsibility (the ability to respond) becomes clearer.

A third step is recognition that as human beings we still have the possibility of choosing a livable future for ourselves and our descendants. A glimpse of hopeful possibilities will make it possible for people to take the first two steps without panic, or what seems to currently exist for many—denial.

Once community with other living things, as well as each other, is truly experienced and appreciated, our way of life, previously taken for granted, becomes unacceptable.

In essence this is a religious vision. The rise of this vision, especially through the influence of ecological and feminist sensitivities, has been one of the great advances of this generation. Only as the vision deepens and spreads is there hope for making changes that are required by the wild facts.

Most of us are not aware that the stresses of our personal lives are directly interconnected with this shift in both our individual and our collective understanding of what reality means. I find it difficult to surrender my position as "superior" to such lowly abstractions as rock and soil, the tundra, or a spruce tree. I admit that they are important, but surely not "equal to."

∽

As I look through my cabin window to the rocky crag of Mount Truth against the turquoise sky of March, I am more conscious than ever that we must find ways to reflect on this great upheaval in our vision. Otherwise we will be swept up into the madness of society's failed vision of reality.

As we must take responsibility for the creation of our own personal philosophy and world view, so must we take responsibility for the creation of the context in which they are lived. For philosophy and theology are not theoretical. They are our values, our ethics—chosen and lived responsibly. Until we accept responsibility for that reality, we will remain trapped in the inevitable assumptions that someone, or something of a higher order, a higher power—God, or Good, or Science, or Mother, or the Great Mystery—will make things all right, will see to it that we will be all right.

∽

Ultimately, the most important wild fact is what the Eskimo calls "koviashuktok." Koviashuktok, or the inner dream, is the outlet. It is one with the living water welling up from the very springs of being that nourish and sustain all life. Without it life becomes a dreary, dead place, and deep within, our spirit begins to rot. The inner dream need not be some great and overwhelming plan; it need not be a dramatic picture of what might or must be some day.

Koviashuktok is the quiet persistence in the heart that enables us to ride out the storms of churning experiences.

Koviashuktok is the exciting whisper moving through the isles of our spirit answering the monotony of limitless days of dull routine. It is the ever-recurring melody in the midst of broken harmony and harsh discords of human conflict. It is the touch of significance which highlights the ordinary experience, the common event, the wonder of each hour, the beauty of the earth.

Koviashuktok is no outward thing. It does not take its rise from the environment in which we move and function. It lives in the inward parts, it is deep within where the issues of life and death are ultimately determined.

We need to keep alive this exciting whisper, for as long as we are koviashuktok, we cannot lose the significance of living.

First Humility

All systems of thought
    that clog our minds with theories
      that ignore this earth
        are counterfeit.
Let us not endure
    a slow poison of words
      until our myths and inventions
      and work and deeds
        hide the source of life.
We are a people of words
    and words are important
      but the first humility
        must be before this earth
        which gives us life
          sustains and feeds us.

Our earth has been photographed from the moon
and we have dipped our hands in the sea
walked over curved hills
listened to the silence
of forests.
Out of the earth we have come,
to ignore it is death.
It is to wager your life.
You bet your life
it is!

A Polar Parable
Of Those Who Care

Now there was a time when the man of Koviashuvik did attend great meetings at the university.

Men and women of affairs gathered from the ends of the earth to make palaver about the land and about those that dwell therein far to the north.

The man of Koviashuvik did listen to many learned papers which did speak of oil and pipelines that cost billions of shekels. Also of roads to the north slope of the Brooks Range.

There also did he observe that many people spoke of their concern for the land. Yea, even the wilderness wherein is found Koviashuvik. Spake they of care for the tundra, even of the caribou for whom they would cause to be built over- and underpasses that they might migrate as of old. Spake they also of many controls and anti-pollution insofar as the wilderness might be preserved.

Then pondered the man of Koviashuvik: "Even so, a wilderness is that place wherein people disturbeth it as little as possible. And yet, no one sayeth to leave the wilderness alone."

Postscript

Your destiny is a mystery to us. What will happen when the buffalo are all slaughtered? The wild horses tamed? What will happen when the secret corners of the forest are heavy with the scent of many men and the view of the ripe hills is blotted by talking wires?

Where will the thicket be? Gone!

Where will the eagle be? Gone! And what is it to say good-bye to the swift pony and the hunt? The end of living and the beginning of survival.

—Chief Seattle in a letter to the U.S. Government

The month of April
has a greater percentage of sunshine
than any other.

April

SPARKLING SNOW CRYSTALS reflect billions of suns beneath a cloudless blue. The glare is blinding. Against a white mountain the black silhouette of a raven gives it dimensional reality. With every fourth beat of glistening black wings, Tulugak sends a metallic, bell-like cry ringing across the frozen lake.

Eskimos say it is his special spring migration voice calling, "Tuktu!" "Caribou!"

On this Easter morning I hear the cry: "It's here! Here!"

Running my hand along a twig, now downy with new pussy willow fuzz, I feel its "inua," the Nunamiut Eskimo term for an essential existing force in living and inanimate objects which gives them meaning.

I hear you brother Tulugak. Spring is here!

Weather

In April, the rapidly lengthening days keep temperatures climbing. By May they will be well above freezing. April is the driest month of the year. It has a greater percentage of possible sunshine than any other month, therefore the danger of snow blindness is ever present.

I had been cutting wood and my sunglasses were a nuisance. They slid with perspiration on the bridge of my nose and the bows rubbed the back of my ears as I swung the heavy double-bit axe. I put the dark glasses in my pocket and forgot about them.

The next morning, when I awakened, I found it difficult to open my eyes. The lids seemed glued together. I was reminded of a case of pink-eye I had in childhood. When I forced my eyes open, the pain was excruciating, as if ground glass rubbed beneath the lids.

There is little one can do for snow blindness except wait it out and immobilize the eyelids as much as possible. We had an analgesic ointment in case of infection or eye injury but this was not an infection. It was sunburned eyeballs through the lids. The whites of my eyes were a frightening red, and the only relief was a cool compress.

A doctor in Fairbanks had cautioned not to use an anesthetic for snow blindness as an eyelash or foreign body would not be felt and serious trouble could result. Home remedies among wilderness dwellers in the Brooks Range are numerous, from using a poultice of moistened dehydrated potatoes to one recommended by an Eskimo woman—boiled Labrador tea.

Like all problems with the weather, prevention is the first consideration. Most mistakes in this climate are made only once. There is not often a second chance.

An Arctic Allegory
Of the Duck Who Set Out Too Soon

When the cold of winter passes, many birds, likewise geese and ducks fly north of the Arctic Circle.

Even unto Koviashuvik do they fly wherein they might mate and bring forth their young during the days of the midnight sun.

Albeit, one duck arrived earlier than the rest. Peradventure he misjudged the time. Ice still remained on the lake and sparse was the water in which to swim. Even so the duck returned not from whence he came.

Then in the night a great storm did blow from the north which caused the ice to shift in diverse ways. The duck became caught in the ice and therein did it perish.

It was after the storm that the man of Koviashuvik found where the duck had perished. And he did mourn its passing for it was of beauty and worth.

Then thinketh he: "So it is in the world of women and men. How often has a thing of beauty or a plan of worth been sent forth before the climate was ready to receive it. Peradventure it too ended up a dead duck."

Myth of Easter

North of the Arctic Circle, Easter is a time of promise more than a time of tradition. Tradition speaks of a triumph of goodness over evil, of truth over expediency, of life over death.

However, it is by the promise of spring that we live confidently through the year ahead and through all the days of our lives. This is the myth of Easter.

With a promise of summer in the swelling buds of willows beyond the lake shore ice, I find it difficult to relate the traditional Christian Easter to this world of nature which Thoreau called wildness.

Most of us do not believe that dead people come back to life. We cannot honestly speak of resurrection from the dead. And yet the theme of Easter, that life and love are stronger than death and hate, has a powerful hold upon us.

Life does renew itself. Spring returns. Hope is continually resurrected in the human heart. Resurrection is one of our most deeply held myths.

We know that myths are not simply imaginary stories or fairy tales. The truth of a myth does not depend upon its being factual. A myth may have very little to do with fact. Here, in this northern fastness on this Easter Sunday, I am acutely aware of the difference between truth and fact.

An author writes a novel, and if it is a great novel, it will portray great truths. The author does not necessarily deal with facts. He or she is writing fiction. However, it may be fiction embodying great truths.

And so it is, not only with Eskimo legends but with traditional Easter stories, from bunnies carrying chocolate eggs to angels sitting in an open tomb. They are not history. They do not deal with facts. But within them sing subjective truths of spring which have sung in people's hearts for centuries and which still find a sympathetic echo in our own at this joyful time.

❧

As a matter of fact, the date of Easter began as a Christianized celebration of the Jewish feast of the Passover. And, as a matter of fact, the Jewish Passover derived from a primitive Semitic tribal celebration of the returning spring which was observed at the first full moon near the time of the vernal equinox.

The facts are that the apostolic church knew nothing of Easter. And, as a matter of fact, the date for Easter was determined in a period when Christianity was in process of becoming the official religion of the ancient Roman world, more than 300 years after Jesus' birth.

We also know the date for Easter was determined during much controversy in 325 AD at the Council of Nicaea. This was the same council which, by a controversial vote, adopted the doctrine of the trinity as the official belief of Christians.

To settle the Easter controversy, the council authoritatively determined that Easter should fall on a Sunday. Then, not only on a Sunday, but the first Sunday following the first full moon on, or the next after, the vernal equinox. In fact, depending upon the moon, Easter can be any Sunday between March 21st and April 25th.

As a matter of fact, the word Easter—Oestre—is the pagan spring goddess of the Norsemen. And, six hundred years before the birth of Jesus, Greek mothers and fathers were telling their children a story to explain why, after the long winter months, the earth suddenly springs to life, and there is rejoicing in its beauty as the people celebrate with songs and dancing.

As a matter of fact, it is pretty well agreed by scholars that it was from the beliefs of the early Christian missionaries that the resurrection concept (that Jesus had risen from the dead) arose. Their message was that all who believe in him and his triumph over death, will, at their own death, share his triumph and live forever.

As a matter of fact, the dead do not rise, and we know it. To believe such a literalism is to indulge in superstition. However, if we know this is not history, but a myth, like an Eskimo story or legend, we can see the poetic truth of life. There is a mystery in the story of life which captivates us.

∽

To read the story of life, from its microscopic origins 500 million years or more ago through the long epochs of geological evolution; and then through the ages of fossils, vertebrates, reptiles, and mammals; then, finally the primates and humans...to read this story and sense its meaning is to feel strength and hope and confidence which is unshakable.

Until now, nothing has been able to stop the onward movement of life. No cataclysm, disaster, or even the old adversary, death, has been able to halt the movement and march of life.

Whether, as in the past, we called it spirit, or vital essence, or inua of the Eskimo, there is something at the heart of life that simply says "no" to individual deaths and which continues from before the age of dinosaurs until today.

To realize that this indomitable force is within us and all around us in every living thing on this earth; to understand that this force motivates our urge for care and concern; to feel this truth to the depths of one's being is to know a power and a strength and faith which are the most sustaining of human experiences.

∽

On the glittering shore of this frozen lake on this April morning I am aware that Easter is the carrier of a truth that has sung in people's hearts for centuries.

Easter takes the stark and ugly realities of life and shapes them into forms, and dresses them in beautiful garments.

Despair becomes hope, sorrow becomes discipline, foul becomes clean, the difficult becomes easy, hardship becomes a challenge, and death itself is swallowed up in victory.

If we look upon life only with the cold eye of reasoned fact there is little inducement for our wanting to continue it.

We came into this world causing pain. Our first cry was a protest. Our childhood is a history of wanting to do things we are not permitted to do, and being forced to do things we don't want to do. We have to go to bed when we are not sleepy and get up when we are sleepy. We have to like people we don't care for (at least pay deference to them). Life is contrariness and frustration.

As adults, if we win fame or fortune (or if we don't) it doesn't matter, really. We have no assurance of happiness in the facts of life.

The facts are, that in a little while our busy brains cease to function and we are gone. In fact, when we begin to live we begin to die. In the midst of life we are in death.

The world rolls on careless of tears. The affairs and activities we thought so important are no longer of moment. From this point of view, our human attainments are of less than microscopic importance. These are the facts.

But, if we crown facts with myth, and feeling with intuition and imagination, how the scene changes!

Birth is a precious pearl, bought at great price. The first cry of a baby is a song of victory. The whole life of the child is a poem, its separate parts written in different meters; always to be concluded and never dull. And through it all runs the motive of aspiration and conquest.

The life of the adult becomes a sacred trust; talents that must not be buried, lights that must not be hidden under a bushel. Life is a romance to each of us greater than the pen has ever portrayed. We may look to others like ordinary, commonplace folks, but each of us knows better. Destiny has whispered to each of us. We have a mission. We are partners in a great drama. Life is a stage on which we play the leading role; we ourselves sit in at the performance, and we are, at the same time, the most critical and appreciative of all the audience. All our little battles become of more importance than any learned sage has ever recounted. We move among trusted friends and comrades. Hardship only makes us strong; disappointment only makes us understanding; sorrow only makes us tolerant. This rough turmoil of life takes on meaning. We feel the dignity of being a person. We feel the divinity of our heritage.

Many peoples, from the ancient Greeks to the inland Eskimo, thought they were descended from gods. We too know we are children of this universe, and all are our brothers and sisters.

∾

Here at Koviashuvik, as I consider the Christian Easter myth, the rise and spread of the teachings of a Palestinian carpenter is one of the wonders of history.

An obscure Jewish teacher was made into a dying and rising savior-hero after the manner of the Mediterranean mystery religions. He was built by the imagination of the church (perhaps because of the need of humble people yearning for beauty) into a royal deity of blinding majesty.

However, the Christ of the church has little to do with an obscure, itinerant preacher of the Galilean lakes. It took a myth, a great, breathtaking myth, to fire the imagination and make Easter the festival that it became.

Here, in this apparently frozen world, a raven's call reminds me that this celebration of joy and beauty is no weak and helpless thing in a hard and brutal world. Easter belongs here, as it has ever been, a cup of strength to our souls. For life is a song if we would but hear its music. Sometimes in it are sounds of springtime, dancing, and silvery waters. Sometimes it is a solemn dirge. But through all of its variations is the strain of affirmation.

Affirmation that is greater than circumstances, joy greater than sorrow—and, above all, that care and concern deep within, which we call love.

A Polar Parable
Of Landmarks

In the days that are remembered there dwelt in the land of the far north those who would seek their fortune in the streambeds of the high mountains.

Dug they in the creeks to bedrock. There they marked the claims wherein they sought gold which would make them rich, even as the rulers of the Medes and the Persians. There also they constructed cabins of logs therein to dwell. And there they did make landmarks wherefore all might know the boundaries of their claims, albeit few claims ever paid for their grubstake.

And the years did pass away even as the moose scats which falleth in the snow. And the cabins did crumble away, and in all the land few did dwell therein.

Then on a certain day there came to the far north a man whose hair was white with the years of four score and three, yet still did he climb the mountains even as a youth.

And when the man of Koviashuvik did inquire of him what he sought, he said: "I seek a creek wherein times past I did pan much gold. I would share with thee if thou would'st help me find the ancient landmark."

Many days did they hike the hills and valleys and over the high passes but they found it not. Perchance someone had aforetimes removed it.

Then the man of Koviashuvik did ponder this, and sayeth to himself: "Among men who seek to find that which they once knew, it is written of old: 'Remove not the ancient landmark which thy fathers have set.'" (Proverbs 22:28)

Postscript

Care of the soul is not solving the puzzle of life; quite the opposite, it is an appreciation of the paradoxical mysteries that blend light and darkness into the grandeur of what human life and culture can be.

—Thomas Moore

> It is not I
> It is life
> that loves
> In me

At break-up the curtain opens,
heralding summer.

May

DURING THE LONG, warm days before break-up snow sinks upon itself. Twilight lasts all night with only the brightest stars dimly visible in a silent world. Last night the silence was broken. I awoke to the sound of gurgling water which grew in volume as rivulet after rivulet joined the cacophony of chirping redpolls in the willow thicket along the creek.

In this morning's sun, iridescent blowflies swarm on the south face of the cabin, adding their high-pitched hum to the sounds, which for the past seven months have been locked in the silent cold.

Great dark, wet fans now creep out across the flat-white surface of the lake from where creeks pour out their overflow.

At creek mouths, buds of balsam poplar trees swell reddish-purple among the bare, white limbs. They swell as if, when they burst, their life songs too might join the chorus.

Even so, this is just a tune-up for the symphony to come, which is now winging north in thousands of migrant birds who will fill the wilderness with their joyful sounds of life.

Here, in this great blue domed auditorium, the curtain has opened heralding summer.

Break-up has arrived!

Weather

Although the actual number of hours of sunshine increases in May, the possible percentage decreases with the increase of cloudy weather. Snow may fall in May. However, near the end of the month light rain showers or sleet are more common. Days become more than twenty hours long and night temperatures are seldom below freezing.

Melting snows begin as trickles in mountain gullies until the rivulets turn to rushing torrents. These pour into frozen rivers, breaking and lifting great chunks of ice. These in turn, with the pressure of the increasing flood, grind away banks with their brush and trees, often changing the river channels and leaving great ice blocks hundreds of yards from the original river bed when the water subsides.

With the melting of snow and ice, millions of insects hatch. New leaves appear on willow, alder, birch, and tacamahac.

Blossoms appear everywhere. Flocks of birds arrive. Their songs and excited cries above the sound of running water fill the warming air.

May is the month of break-up.

An Arctic Allegory
Of Good Terns

And behold, there came in the spring of the year to the far north diverse birds wherein they might build their nests and lay their eggs and thus be fruitful and multiply.

On the shores of Koviashuvik many birds did find their mates and marked their boundaries wherein they would raise their broods in the land of midnight sun.

And among those who did arrive at Koviashuvik with a flutter of wings and cries of gladness was an arctic tern who had flown 11,000 miles from Tierra del Fuego, at the other end of the earth.

Even so, this fine bird of exquisite beauty did arrive alone. His mate flew not with him to their land of joy, peradventure she had been consumed by a great eagle or lost at sea.

Each day the man of Koviashuvik and the woman of wisdom did watch this splendid tern as he graced the air with translucent wings in the sunshine and dived for small fish in sparkling waters. Yet their hearts were saddened for they did observe that he was alone.

And it came to pass, when the shadows were long, that another fine tern did arrive at Koviashuvik from the end of the earth. And she also was a fowl of grace and beauty, who swept with curved wings the blue of heaven. And the two birds did find each other wherefore all was fulfilled.

Then the man of Koviashuvik said to the woman of wisdom: "So it has ever been. One good tern deserves another."

Break-up and the Days to Come

Instead of a gentle spring at Koviashuvik, break-up arrives like an avalanche.

Rivers roar. Birds fill valleys with song. Ducks and geese call. Loons laugh on lakes. Arctic terns and falcons hover over myriad ponds glistening with the iridescent wings of newly hatched insects.

Summer comes with plunging waterfalls and hanging green valleys. In the central mountains a white Dall sheep stands motionless on a pinnacle of rock high above turbulent water. Great white clouds billow above blue mountains until they are dark with rain, sleet and hail. Lightning ignites fires and smoke drifts up valleys where clouds of mosquitoes hum among the muskeg's cotton-grass sedges. Fireweed is crimson in the foothills, and by mid-June the sun never sets but just touches the horizon between sunset and sunrise.

With the first frosts of autumn, mountains sing with orange alder, yellow willow, and golden birches. Antlers flash white as a moose lifts its dripping head from the marsh. A grizzly bear, golden brown in the sun, fattens on blueberries where flocks of ptarmigan share the bounty of cloudberries and scarlet lingonberries.

By October the cold seals rivers and creeks. Stars glitter above crags no one has climbed. There echoes down canyons the howl of wolves at their kill. The aurora twists, turns, and dances across the sky above a now quiet range. Birds have trained their young and flown south, leaving only Alaska jays and chickadees to watch the frost flowers form on icy marshes and frozen ponds.

Now is silence.

Cobalt-blue mountains tower into a turquoise sky where stars appear in mid-afternoon and the only sound is the clicking of a thousand hooves as a herd of caribou crosses the ice.

In midwinter the range is a prehistoric land, motionless except for the aurora streaming overhead. The only boundary, it seems, is the stars.

This is Koviashuvik—a word to encompass a mountain range and its life without diminishing it, bringing it into a focus of meaning. Impossible to speak of except in terms of seasons, for the cycles are always ending and beginning.

Soon after break-up, millions of excited birds arrive. The arctic terns fly 11,000 miles from Antarctica for courtship and mating here.

Voices are everywhere. The door of silence bursts open with running water and bird songs. In the swollen creeks rocks tumble, and my axe is a beat to the harmony of white-crowned sparrows in the willows.

From Koviashuvik an inner call has been heard by multitudes of migrating waterfowl. Loons, swans, cranes, plovers, geese, and ducks by the thousands arrive at the place of their year's fulfillment.

No one knows why this range calls so many animals that move with the seasons. Perhaps in a warmer age the animal center of population was here, and its descendants have an urge to return. Perhaps it is because the north has been a place apart. Or, perhaps it is for them, as for me, a response to the place itself, a place where there is a fresh crispness in the air and the sun shines night and day to circle the horizon instead of climbing over the zenith so that light and shadow always have the fresh touch of morning.

Perhaps beyond light and shadow, the great blue range is still carrying a message difficult to hear in the confusions of today's crowded world, a message that there is still a place and time of joy if we but seek it.

Kia

The fox adopted us at the end of April.

I say adopted us, because he joined us on his terms, not ours. Although he would occasionally take a piece of caribou from my hand, he never let me touch him. His independence was always evident even when he romped around the cabin and put on a show for us by chasing his tail and rolling in the snow. We considered him our pet, but actually we were his.

❧

I was first aware of his presence when I observed his tracks paralleling my snowshoe trail along the frozen lake shore. There had been no sign of fox during the winter. I thought the tracks might be those of a coyote. Coyotes have been reported to occasionally wander this far north. His curiosity was evident. He checked out all of my wolverine and wolf snares and the places where I had cut and stacked dry wood. He had even left a stain in the snow next to the spot where I had performed the same function the day before.

When I returned to the cabin, I discovered that the fox had also been there. He had explored our trails to the cache, storage shed, and woodpile. I noted that he carefully avoided crossing the paths made by our snowshoes. Only when necessary had he leaped over our trails to continue on the other side.

"I think we have a coyote in the vicinity," I told Nuliak, as I hung up my parka and began removing my mukluks. "The tracks are much too small for a wolf, and he is wise to the snares."

Before I had my second mukluk removed, she said, "Look out there!" Pointing to the cabin window she said, "There it is. It's a fox!"

Standing just outside the cabin window on a snowdrift in the glow of the lamp light, Reynard was poised, motionless, watching us. His golden eyes showed no fear, only curiosity. Then, turning toward the front of the cabin he walked out of sight.

We quickly opened the door. And again, in the light which streamed across the snow, he stopped and curiously looked us over from about twenty-five feet away before continuing down the hill into the dark.

⌒◡

The next morning, Reynard (or Vixen—we were not sure) was nosing among the scraps where we threw our kitchen midden down the hill. He glanced at us to be sure a proper distance was being kept, but otherwise went about his business of digging out a morsel, then carrying it a short distance across the snow and burying it.

He would dig a hole with his paws and then drop the scrap or piece of bone into the depression. Then, by pushing snow over it with his nose, cover it.

I cut a piece of raw meat from a caribou leg hanging in the cabin entryway and tossed it near him, calling, "Here, Reynard—Vixen. Try this!"

He ignored my call and gesture. Then he caught the scent of the meat. Sniffing out the piece I had tossed, he picked it up, trotted down the hill several yards and buried it. Then, walking over to a willow stem projecting from the snow, he sniffed it on both sides and urinated on it.

He was not a Vixen. With this gesture, the fox seemed to claim the territory and with it, he adopted us. We called him Kia, an Eskimo term spoken as a question and translated as, whose is it?

❧

Kia was a handsome red fox with dark socks and white chest which matched the tip of his long bushy tail. In the Brooks Range, this fox has several color phases, from the usual red, like Kia, to the black, exotic silver fox with its white, silver-tipped tail. Those neither red nor black are referred to as cross fox. The Alaskan red fox occurs frequently in the cross phase, more commonly in the red phase, but only rarely in the silver or black.

Like the lynx, the fox increase in numbers during those periods when snowshoe hares, voles, and other small animals are numerous. This occurs in a cycle of about ten to twelve years.

These animal cycles are characteristic phenomena of the subarctic and arctic. Regularly spaced periods of great abundance of particular animals are followed by sudden decreases. These "crashes" seem to occur in a single season. As a local trapper once told me, "It can ruin you! All of a sudden there's no fox or lynx when the winter before they were all over the place."

Trappers monitor hare populations. When they crash, lynx and fox disappear with them. We noticed that there was an obvious increase in the number of snowshoe or varying hares this past winter. Kia's appearance was a response to this increase. We could expect more fox as well as lynx next autumn.

∾

Kia followed my trail wherever I went, keeping at a distance and usually out of sight. Whenever I returned from cutting wood or from an exploratory hike of several miles, I found his tracks paralleling mine. Seldom would he cross my trail. When he did so, he always jumped over it.

I was as curious about him as he was about me. I would double back to a vantage point where I could watch him following my track. Occasionally he would leave it to explore and hunt, but then return to my trail.

Not only did he obviously have a keen sense of smell, but I observed that his sight and hearing were equally acute. Following my trail, he would suddenly break away from it where a shrew had crossed the track of my snowshoes to scurry on under the snow.

Kia would walk slowly along on the thin crust with his nose down until he apparently heard the small creature below. Then, tipping his head to one side, he would listen, then tip it to the other. When he had located the shrew's exact position, he would shuffle his feet into a preparatory crouch, then pounce, coming down through the snow in an attempt to pin the tiny animal under his front feet. If the shrew escaped the pounce, there was a flurry of snow as the fox scrambled after it. I observed that he usually caught his prey.

∽

One morning, on my way to cut and stack some dead spruce trees to be sledded later to the cabin, I passed several winter-white, willow ptarmigan, invisible in the snow except for the dark pin-points of their eyes. They huddled, still, about twenty feet up the hill from me. I was curious to see whether Kia would see or smell them. Continuing along the mountain side about a quarter of a mile, I stopped on a rise which projected in such a manner that I could look back along the way I had come.

With my field glasses, I scanned the area where I had seen these northern mountain grouse. I soon spotted a cock, picking on buds at the base of a clump of willows. I saw him because his winter coat of white was already becoming mottled with new, brown, summer feathers making him easy to see against the snow from my vantage point above him. There was no sign of Kia.

As I watched, the ptarmigan moved down the hill to another willow bush close to my trail where they disappeared in the thicker undergrowth. Through the glasses, I traced the path made by my snowshoes to where it disappeared over a ridge. There was still no sign of the fox. Perhaps he was hunting elsewhere and not following my trail today.

I put down my field glasses and picked up the axe to cut a dead tree. As I raised the axe my eye caught a movement in spruce below the place where the ptarmigan had disappeared. I quickly picked up the binoculars to see what it was. It was Kia, covering something in the snow with long forward pushing strokes with his nose.

When he finished, he turned along the track my snowshoes had made and began trotting toward me. Although I was downwind from him and did not move, he sensed my presence. He stopped and stood with his bushy tail erect, as red fox do when tense or excited. He then left the trail and circled out of sight up the mountain side into the trees above me. I did not see him again that day.

After cutting and stacking dead wood for a couple of hours, I snowshoed down the slope to where Kia had buried something in the snow. It was a cock ptarmigan, probably the one I had been watching. Its head had been eaten but the rest of its frozen body was intact. I carried it back to the cabin where we had Kia's ptarmigan for supper. It gave us a variation in our diet of caribou and we considered it a fair exchange for our contribution of caribou to Kia.

∾

Although the red fox in its various color phases is the only fox commonly found in the Brooks Range, the white arctic fox has been known to occasionally enter the mountains. The arctic fox prefers open terrain north of timberline and occurs in great numbers along the arctic coast, particularly in years when lemmings are abundant.

Trappers have taken arctic foxes on the southern slope of the range, but as the Eskimo hunter Elijah Kakinya told me, "This not his home. He live near the ocean. He only here because he get lost."

The red fox is at home throughout the range. In the timberless north they are found in terrain that is broken by rocks, small hills, and riverbanks. On the southern slope he and his mate usually dig their dens on sunny knolls in the open. Only occasionally is a den made in the woods.

The den, which is commonly a burrow with several entrances, often began as the home of ground squirrels, or "parky" squirrels, as they are called by the Eskimos who often make their parkas from these squirrel skins. The parky squirrel's burrow may be initially dug out by the pair of foxes in their attempt to catch a parky squirrel. Then it is later enlarged for denning purposes. Dens may be used for several years. A vixen will inspect several before one is chosen, or a new one dug out in April or May.

The fox pups, four to seven in number, are born in late May or early June. During the nursing period of three to five weeks, the vixen is brought food by her mate, who is busily hunting hares, ptarmigan, voles, shrews, and other small animals. He sometimes travels as far as six or seven miles from the den.

❧

I had considered Kia to be a bachelor, as his were the only fox tracks I had seen in the vicinity while the late spring snow remained. I had wondered about the scraps he had buried and dug up, but never suspected that he was caring for a mate. He appeared at the cabin less frequently as the sun melted the snow from all but the surrounding peaks, until one day we were aware that we had seen no sign of him for several weeks.

With snow gone, tracks were recognizable only in the silt along stream bottoms and along the sandy spit of the lake shore. There I discovered fresh fox tracks preceding me in the sand one afternoon, and looking up along the shore of the lake I saw a pair of foxes trotting together. They were less than a quarter of a mile away and I recognized one of them as Kia. The pair disappeared around a point without looking back.

On a hunch, I explored the canyon above the place where I had seen them disappear. There I found their den. It appeared to have been recently abandoned. Kia had a mate and family all the time he was with us.

Where were the pups? Were they with the parents but not in sight? I never knew.

This was my last contact with Kia. We assumed that he and his family moved on to other parts.

⌒

That was over a year ago. And since it snowed last night, I hiked along the shore of the lake to read the tracks of animals which had been moving about after the blizzard. As I returned to pick up my trail through the spruce trees, I saw the tracks of a fox. He had paused at a stump where I had stopped earlier and left his stain next to mine in the snow. His tracks paralleled mine to within a hundred yards of the cabin, then turned down the slope and across the creek to disappear in the forest.

When I entered the cabin, my first words were, "Kia is back!"

We have discovered that it is not the same fox. But Kia is back. Yes, he really is.

Out of the Darkness

Out of the darkness
    of grief and
    of dying,
Out of defeat,
    of battles unwon,
Again and again
    as earth turns
    in orbit

Born and reborn
with wings
in the sun,
A song of thanksgiving
soars up
in the morning,
The spirit of life
with a race
to be run.

A Polar Parable
Of That Which is Exposed

Now for many days, even those that exceedeth half a year, did the man of Koviashuvik and the woman of wisdom fling forth their slops down the hill in the snow. There the slops did freeze, albeit the snow kept all covered and the beauty of the land remained unchanged.

Then it came to pass that the days of warmth did come to Koviashuvik and the snow did melt and exposed that which had been covered.

And the man of Koviashuvik did beat his breast, saying: "Woe is me. Not only doth it appear unsightly with eggshells, bones, and diverse bits and pieces, peradventure it also stinketh and the flies increase in numbers as the sands on the shore of the distant sea."

Then as he labored with pick and shovel to cover that which had been exposed, he thought: "So it is among the multitude. There comes a time when that which stinketh is exposed wherein even a shovel doeth no good."

Postscript

On some days it is good to be a tree looking in all directions at once.
On some days it is better to be a rock saying nothing and blind to everything.

When life becomes too hard here I become an eagle and fly away to see how small the earth really is, then I can laugh and come back home again.

—Taos Pueblo Indian saying

Jeff Whaley photo

*Twenty-four hours
of daylight.*

June

ON THIS LONGEST DAY of the year there is no sunrise this far north. Yesterday's sun never set. Stars will not be seen for at least two months.

Birds sing continually, seeming never to roost. Growth of willows and the hatching of insects is frenetic. Mosquitoes rise like smoke from the marshy tundra along the lake shore. High-finned grayling swim in the shallows to feed on insects which touch down on glistening water to lay their eggs. Ring after rippling ring expands on the lake. These distort the immense mirror of mountains as a grayling's high dorsal fin breaks the surface.

The mirror erupts with a roiling splash. Swirling water shatters the tranquillity. A golden-sided lake trout returns to the depths with a ten-inch grayling still flexing in its stomach.

As I watch the greater circle expand across the glinting water, a mosquito swells red on the back of my hand. I brush it off and think of circles as I fasten a lure to my fish line.

Tonight I shall have mosquitoes and grayling in the form of lake trout for supper. And tomorrow the earth will swing back again toward the sunless days of winter to form another circle.

What is a circle?

The dictionary calls it "A series ending where it began and perpetually repeated."

So do I.

Weather

In June, temperatures can occasionally reach ninety degrees. Freezing temperatures are rare. In mid-June there is no night and the sun never sets below the horizon. Increasing showers give more than twice the precipitation of May, which modifies the sunlight.

From miles away, lightning-started fires can create enough smoke to limit local visibility to less than a quarter of a mile.

Mosquitoes are at their worst, rising from the soggy muskeg in clouds.

Melting snow and permafrost fill every creek and streambed. From rivulets to torrents, the moisture circles back seeking the tranquillity of lakes and the sea.

An Arctic Allegory
Of Splashing Fish

It was in those days, when the ice had gone from the lake and the sun set not, that the man of Koviashuvik and the woman of wisdom did stand before their cabin on the shore at midnight, wherein the beauty of the day remaineth.

There they heard splashing fish, and there they listened to the cry of an arctic tern and the laughter of a loon.

Also, they watched a great fish make circles in the water as it rose to feed upon an insect which floated upon the surface.

Then observed the man of Koviashuvik: "So it is in the world of women and men. The great fish only roil the surface while the small fish make a loud splash."

What Does it Mean?

As I watched circles expand on the quiet surface of the lake, I asked myself, what is the "meaning" of a circle? Does it have meaning beyond a geometric form?

I am not referring to definitions which we usually think of, such as, "A circle is a plane curve everywhere equidistant from a fixed point." I am thinking of a circle as an idea. Ideas and their implications probe deep into the human spirit. What does a circle mean?

Among other things, a circle means an infinite number of points absolutely the same distance from a certain point. This seems a simple idea. A circle is an idea. Now, how big is a circle?

When I say an infinite number of points, the first thing I face is the idea of infinity. Infinity is a big idea. People have not always had it.

Then there is this idea of a point. That is also a big idea. It is the idea of one, the indivisible. Theologically it has been called monotheism. Monotheism is the idea of one, the indivisible.

A circle also means no beginning and no end. This is forever, eternal, everlasting.

Now, another thing. Set that infinite, indivisible, eternal circle in motion—a wheel which moves point after infinite circumference point. How long then before these infinite number of points will begin to repeat themselves? And, if they do, if the wheel really goes around, and the points are really infinite, can infinity repeat itself on into infinity?

Or, what about the axis point? Does it turn around also? If it does, then part is up while the other part is down, or part is facing east while the rest faces west, and anything that can face two ways at once has two or more sides and is no point!

The axis then cannot be said to move at all.

At the center of infinite motion we have the paradox of infinite stillness. This is a concept mystics and artists have tried to convey. "At the still-point in the center of the circle one can see the infinite in all things." (Chuang-tsu)

As I watched an expanding circle break up the still reflection of a mountain peak, I saw it as an art form.

Art has been called the universal language. From the most ancient times, our forebears unconsciously, as well as with intention, employed art techniques to convey ideas and emotions, particularly religious ideas and emotions.

In the universal language of art, pictures and sculpture may be regarded as symbols, as signs, or maps. However, no map is the territory or even a true copy of it. Every individual word in a passage of prose or poetry can no more be said to denote some specific reference than does every brush stroke of every line in a painting have its counterpart in reality.

It is the same with speech. Like painting, words are representations. The function of speech is to stimulate and set up thoughts in us having correspondence with the speaker's thoughts and concerns. The speaker has not transmitted a copy of his or her thoughts, only submitted a substitute, made from the uncompromising material of sound.

The musician, painter, sculptor, and writer are all akin in this. They make representations of their thoughts, feelings, ideas, moods, using their chosen limited materials. In a sense, nature does the same thing. A person may appreciate a work of art, but unless he or she undergoes some transformation as a result, unless she or he undergoes somewhat the experience of the artist, the pattern did not connect.

The creation of the artist has form, or pattern, inasmuch as it represents a continuity of her or his experience. It has form so long as it obeys certain patterns or rules. It has meaning for us only if it represents a continuity, an extension of our own experience. This is probably why Chinese music seems so strange to me although Chinese music fits the definition of music as "order in sound and time." There is something about the concept of order that gives meaning to our observations, both inner and outer.

In the Judeo-Christian-Muslim myth of creation, order might be considered the second step in creation and the first one available to people. Out of the void, chaos. Out of chaos, order. On this longest day in June, when the sun never sets behind the mountains, I ask myself: What is the meaning of order out of chaos?

It might be called wholeness, which has the same root word as holiness.

What is meant by wholeness? In a sense, wholeness is not whole if we think of it as stationary. Like a ripple on the lake, it is not complete unless it also is somehow in motion. That is, unless it works, unless it moves through space or time; in the language of poetry, through our hearts or through our spirits.

Usually we think of pattern, or order, as though it were life-less, aloof, impersonal. This is an understandable reaction to the mechanistics of our twentieth century civilization. Within the realm of what has been called spirit, pattern may well be not only that which in-forms, but that which in-spires, which breathes into. The breath of life.

If music is defined as order in sound and time, what does it mean when heard as a song from an arctic loon or as the rhythmic slap of waves along the water's edge?

Music, as we know its pattern here in the west, orders pitch by prescribing only twelve frequencies out of the myriad of those that are perceptible to our ears. The pattern, the rules of organization of these pitches, it calls harmony. And the color of sound is ordered by prescribing mechanisms for producing these tones, such as vibrating strings, vibrating columns of air, or a vibrating surface such as a drum or cymbal. With all of these tones and instruments, western civilization has organized the loudest and most varied musical instrument ever heard, the symphony orchestra. With today's electronics, there is apparently no limit.

However, the patterns that connect us remind us that more can be said by a flute, or a white-crowned sparrow, in a few minutes than the grandest operatic forces in two hours.

Music is essentially a time art. Time is its canvas or clay. Music gives shape, pattern, beauty, and meaning to time. Its tempo attempts to relate the speed with which rhythm and sound move through time. At what pace can one pass through how much time? Or, how fast can one live how long? Hours are not the same length; only by definition. No two minutes are ever of equal duration.

There is music in this moment, on this longest day of the year north of the Arctic Circle. There is an endlessness—ages of stillness and breathless understanding before the circle again turns in its infinite swing from here to there.

What is it Worth?

At this time of year we watch the migrating birds return to nest. Today something new flew into the area.

A helicopter clattered down on the lake shore where a pair of arctic terns had their nest. The eggs vanished in the air wash. It is late in the season. I hope the scenery of the 11,000 miles they flew to raise their brood was worth the trip. In the circle of life, they are only one pair. They seem to hold no grudge with the chopper pilot. Neither do I. He wouldn't know an arctic tern if he saw one. He told me so. He brought four men from an Alaska oil company to fish for trout.

We also fish for trout from the shore of our isolated lake. And though we hunt and fish for food, there is also a relationship to these rituals which transcends the act.

Another helicopter arrived with an aluminum boat slung beneath it. The skiff was soon loaded with fishing gear and a case of beer. As the outboard motor whined out across the lake, I said to the helicopter pilot, who was having a cup of coffee with me, "Hope they don't toss the empties into the lake."

"They'll bring the cans back," the chopper pilot said. "We've been given the word on pollution. I have to fly out all the empty fuel cans we bring in. I've even picked up some that other guys have left."

The helicopter pilot and his mechanic sat with me for over an hour in front of our cabin on the shore. As we sipped our coffee, conversation ranged from flying conditions in the mountains to changes that the oil fields north of the Brooks Range and the Trans-Alaska pipeline had brought to the wilderness.

"Its kind of a shame," the mechanic said, "that they found all this oil where they did. It'll keep bringing a lot of people in here. Hunting and fishing probably won't be like it used to." He flicked his filter-tipped cigarette butt onto the sandy shore. "Anyhow it'll develop the country. Now that they've opened the road up to the north slope oil fields a lot more people can appreciate what's here."

"Yeah," the pilot said. "Even if you wanted to, you can't stop progress."

∽

Progress can be defined in many ways, I thought, as I stood up and poured fresh coffee. For us, progress had been defined by our move toward a simpler existence, where we had a more immediate connection with the essentials of our lives.

The rising howl of the second helicopter, which had brought in the boat, drowned our conversation. It had taken off without shutting down its engine. Skimming low along the shore, it circled the lake before rising over the mountains and out of sight.

I commented about a pair of loons who had a nest in the path of the mechanical flying crane. "They must have suffered what insurance lawyers call nervous upset," I said to my guests. They both chuckled as if my comment was a joke on the loons.

"Talk about nervous upset!" the mechanic said. "You should have seen a grizzly bear a few days ago up in the pass where they are reworking the road. When the chopper came down over him, it literally scared the shit out of him. He let go at every jump for 200 yards!"

"I had that problem once when I was flying a chopper in Vietnam," the pilot said.

We all laughed.

◦◦◦

An arctic tern hovered in the air above the shallows a hundred yards down the shore from us. It dived into the water, rose with beating wings, and dived again. It was apparently successful in securing a small fish, for it flew off across the lake in its zigzagging flight until it disappeared against the backdrop of mountains.

"I guess you get to see a lot of birds and animals," the pilot said. "It is sure pretty here."

"Yes," I said. "It is."

What an understatement, I thought. "Pretty."

But is there any prism of words that can capture that experience of gazing upon the earth and sky with a wonder and sense of the glimmerings of meaning in the universe?

"What you need up here is a helicopter," the pilot said. "Of course a guy can't afford one unless he's rich, but if you had a chopper, you'd have it made."

"You ought to get one of those ATV's. They only cost a few thousan' dollars," the mechanic said. "I saw an ad for a new model with a caterpillar tread that'll go nearly anywhere. It'll even go into the water and you could use it for fishing, and in the winter it's as good as a snowmobile."

❧

I picked up a chip of wood and took out my pocketknife. Then I began shaving the chip as I wondered how to communicate to these visitors. They did not understand when I told them we had deliberately chosen not to bring in an all-terrain vehicle. I then talked about the difficulty of getting fuel, the noise the engine makes, which would frighten wild animals away, the problem of a breakdown away from the cabin at sub-zero temperatures. These they understood, and for these they quickly came up with suggested solutions.

"If you chartered a large plane for all your supplies, it wouldn't cost you any more to bring in several drums of fuel....They make real quiet engines nowadays....You could keep parts handy."

I tried to point out that these were not the issue.

"It sounds like you're living kind of like the native people used to," the mechanic said. "I'd like to try it sometime. That's why I took this job, to do some hunting and fishing and get out into nature."

The helicopter pilot looked at his watch and stood up. "We'd better be on our way," he said to the mechanic. "We've got to pick up the crew at the drill rig before noon."

He looked at the clouds piled up above the mountains across the lake. "It sure is pretty here," he said again, before walking toward the machine with its great drooping metal blades.

Before climbing into the helicopter they turned and said, "Thanks for the coffee."

"I'll take your mail out when I come back to pick up the guys fishing," the pilot said. "I sure do envy you here."

The starting roar of the helicopter drowned out the whine of the outboard motor in the distance. Reflected in the curved plastic window of the chopper, a pair of arctic terns flew against the sky above the peaks across the lake.

◦‿

How much is an arctic tern worth? What gives it value?

The tern points up the conflict between people's use of the earth and the needs of creatures and plants which occupy it along with them. Where the arctic tern builds its nest there are no restrictions on helicopters and all-terrain vehicles. But many nesting grounds of ducks and geese have been carefully restricted. Once a resource has proved its dollar value, we know what to do. Wild ducks are fun to hunt and trout to catch. A large sportsman's business is dependent upon there being ducks and game fish. Game animals have been pampered. But the arctic tern, like a poem, has dubious cash value. Until we accept some other basis for value, or other rationale, there is little point in discussing its preservation.

◦‿

With the warming up of its engine, the blades of the helicopter began to bite into the air, flattening the willows on the shore, and blowing leaves across the tundra. With an increasing roar and clatter, the machine slowly rose and turned, sweeping away across the lake, roiling the water with the air of its passing.

∼

How do you measure the value of a mountain, a swamp, a desert, an arctic wilderness—the so-called wastelands in which physical barriers have, until now, kept humans and their ingenuity from penetrating?

In retrospect, there is no question of their value. But what was the worth of Walden Pond in 1854? The Judean wilderness before the first century? Sinai before the third month of the Exodus?

∼

At the end of the day, the two helicopters returned to pick up the boat and fishermen. The empty beer cans were brought back, along with a boatload of fourteen lake trout. Three or four of the fish were fifteen-pound patriarchs. It would take a quarter of a century to reproduce them with their slow growth in the icy water of the lake.

"I can't wait 'til the drill crew sees these babies," one of the fishermen said, as he lifted a sack of fish into the chopper. "Every guy there will wish he could get here!"

As the pounding roar of the helicopters faded beyond the hills, I began picking up the cigarette filter tips in front of the cabin. They were really nice guys, thoughtful in their way. They had taken our mail and the pilot brought us a bag of fresh fruit when he returned. They also left us the unused fuel from their outboard motor.

Still I was glad they were gone.

A sandpiper bobbed along the shore, feeding. A loon called from across the lake. It was again as it was...or was it?

Hold Fast the Time

Time has no divisions.
Its quality is sacred
only as we live it,
Not measured by the ticks
of clocks
Or the beat of hearts.
No divisions in time.

A Polar Parable
Of Him Who Would Develop the Land

It came to pass, when the sun returned, that the birds flew north to build their nests in the midst of the wilderness wherein they dwelt. And so did he fly north who would develop the land.

There did he glide his float plane down on the waters of the beautiful lake upon whose shore dwelt the man of Koviashuvik and the woman of wisdom.

And there did the woman of wisdom and the man of Koviashuvik make the visitor welcome. And they set before him a cup of coffee and caribou stew. Also they served him sourdough chocolate cake baked by the woman of wisdom.

After the visitor had partaken, the man of Koviashuvik inquired: "What brings thee to these parts? Perchance to catch the great trout which swim in the lake?"

"Nay," replied the visitor. "I am he who would develop the land. This place hath great beauty and I would construct a lodge near thee so thou mayest prosper from those who would come to catch the great trout. Even so, others will come to dwell in the land, and in this good fortune no longer shalt thou be alone."

The man of Koviashuvik said: "The woman of wisdom and I hath settled here to be alone."

The man who would develop the land said: "Wouldst thou not have a lodge near thee?"

And the man of Koviashuvik responded: "Nay."

Then he who would develop the land said: "Even so, there are other lakes, albeit I comprehendeth not why thou sayest nay. Speak to me the reason?"

Then the man of Koviashuvik answered him saying: "As it was written by Isaiah of old, 'Woe unto them that join house to house, that they lay field to field, till there be no place alone in the midst of the earth.'"

Postscript

Mystical vision is seeing how extraordinary the ordinary is.

—James P. Carse

*The Woman of Wisdom
and the
Man of Koviashuvik.*

July

THE MOUNTAIN TOPS are dusted with snow this late July morning. There is a crisp clarity in the air. This is the first reminder that wood must be stacked before winter and the cabin has to be rechinked.

Yesterday's storm washed away the smoke of forest and tundra fires which drifted up the valleys.

Today the world is re-created fresh and new. It is again the sixth day when "God saw everything that he had made, and, behold it was very good."

Looking above the peaks into a bright blue, the moon is dimly visible. I wonder what the astronauts saw of the earth here, near the top of the world, when they returned from the surface of the moon?

They left a plaque to mark a historic landing, and symbolically froze the event in history for all time to come.

But life is process, not a frozen event. I shall leave no plaque to mark the place on this planet where I too step today for the first time.

Weather

With a mean temperature close to sixty degrees, July has even heavier showers with thunderstorms than June.

Like the thunderstorms of the southwestern United States, as much as an inch of rain can fall in a limited area in half an hour. In these mid-summer storms, rivers and streams can rise three to six feet in a few hours.

An open gravel bar beside a stream is often selected for a campsite because there is usually a breeze and it is freer of mosquitoes. However, it is never wise to camp on such a bar when a storm is in the mountains above. Icy water can isolate and cut off the campsite in the center of a rushing torrent before the danger is evident.

By the end of July, trees, shrubs, and wild flowers are lush, having reached the peak of their short season of growth. Blueberries, lingonberries, cloudberries, and currants are ripe. Bull moose begin rubbing the velvet from their antlers and ptarmigan chicks are learning how to fly.

An Arctic Allegory
Of Questions and the Ways of Caribou

Now it came to pass that a youth did visit Koviashuvik. And he did inquire of many diverse things. Even as to why a caribou lieth down with its front end first and not that which followeth, also that it riseth first with that which followeth?

And the man of Koviashuvik did ponder this, saying: "All animals with warm blood, albeit those with four legs doth so."

Then the youth said, "Nay, the horse riseth first on its front legs!"

The man of Koviashuvik was confused because he had not previously considered this matter, and he said to the youth: "My son, it is the nature of animals to do those things in diverse ways. Even so, do I pull on my right boot before my left, while another doth pull on the left before the right."

Then did he speak of the ways of many creatures. Of the arctic terns which fly each year from the other end of the earth to build their nests at Koviashuvik. Spake he long and wandered in the desert places where no answer could be found and then came he again to the place whence he departed.

Then hearing the sound of his own palaver, the man of Koviashuvik called a halt to his much talking, saying: "Thou art observant my son. I have spent years, peradventure a lifetime, seeing the ways of nature and have considered not what thou didst discover."

Then thinketh the man of Koviashuvik: "So it has ever been. The wise asketh a question while those that know not maketh much wind."

Desert Theology

In terms of rainfall, Koviashuvik could be called a desert. Our precipitation here is about eight inches a year. This is comparable to the deserts of southern Arizona and California. It is the permafrost, the frozen ground, that keeps water from seeping below the surface. The tundra above remains moist, often soggy. So what do we mean by desert?

∽

Theology is an attempt to deal with meaning and the environment in which it finds expression. Paradoxically, this also includes that which separates, alienates, and isolates people from the environment in which they live and have their being.

Experiences are both subjective and objective and come in bits and pieces which are not naturally sorted out in orderly fashion. Dealing with the assortment of experiences a person receives inevitably produces distortions as new experiences are acquired. Thus theologies come and go.

Theology grows out of the question, upon what grounds is action taken? We need not look to ancient theologies in the past to know this. Always, a re-creation is in order.

∽

When I was professor in a graduate theological seminary in Berkeley, California, I drove to the Mojave Desert to live off the land alone. Why? Upon what grounds was this action taken? What was learned?

The first entry in my journal was made approximately sixty-five miles west of Needles, California, and about ninety miles southwest of Las Vegas, Nevada.

It was in this month, July.

July 17: "In the beginning God created the heavens and the earth."
It was after dark when I arrived at the granite boulders which marked the Jeep trail to my abode beneath these junipers. Not bothering to build a fire, I ate the few fresh apricots I had with me, threw my ground cloth down in a sandy wash in the moonlight, and fell asleep.

I awoke once to hear a coyote yapping and noted that moonlight reflecting on my white legs attracted moths. Were they yucca moths, I wondered? The sky was misty silver through the branches, and the ground was hard beneath....(The heavens and the earth).

This particular area, at midsummer was chosen because to many it is the most forbidding. The highway map had advice, boxed in a red square, "Note: Do not turn off main highways on to desert roads without first making local inquiry."

For me however, this area with its many elevations, plants, and animals was far from forbidding. But the Mojave Desert in midsummer did mean that I would be alone.

Why would I want to be alone and seek such a so-called wilderness?

I suppose my answer is the same as all those who have sought solitude from time immemorial. It is not easy to phrase with any accuracy in our day of psychological sophistication. It is the need to step back and take a long look, so ages can speak to the hours.

July 18: "And God called the light Day, and the darkness he called Night. And the evening and the morning were the first day."
Awakened this morning by bussing flies which were singing before the sun rose over the mesa—two kinds of flies, with two different voices. Is the buzz of insect wings a song?

Brewed some Desert Tea, (*Ephedra virdis*), using dry stems. I'll try the other species, (*E. nevadensis*), later. It's a good start for the day, tastes much like regular black tea. Boiled some Old Man Prickly Pear, (*Opuntia erinacea*), then cut a staff from a Canyon Live Oak for poking and food gathering—carved a groove on one end to take snakes and lizards—alive if necessary. Constructed a throwing stick from the same wood for rabbits and birds. This is hopefully the last use of my pocket knife. I shall try to find some obsidian or chert to make cutting tools from now on.

This is general orientation day, so checked on a spring-seep I remembered on a topographic map as a possible camping area. After walking in, found it too dry and baked an exposure in the southwestern sun.

Filling my water container, I drove to the lower desert below lava cliffs. Hiking up a canyon several miles looking for a seep, I discovered many ancient petroglyphs in the lava. Exploring the area, I found an ancient cave-cache with a few pieces of broken pottery. Terribly hot—the four mile hike in 120 degree sun on dark lava was too much—sick when back at the Jeep—no appetite—drank too much water and threw it all up. Finally got to sleep when the flies went to roost. Dragonflies which had lured me with the possibility of water were annoying in the dusk, as five or six flapped their wings with a dry clatter over me. Small ants were irritating, crawling over legs and body. Loose bowels and several vomits helped after the sun went down—then, blessed sleep in the sandy wash below lava cliffs. Except for ants waking me occasionally and a distant coyote call, it was quiet. The stars and milky way were dim in the moonlight and the night breeze was brisk. Finally turned around in the wash so the breeze was at my feet for better sleep.

Thought of the Indians who had slept here many years before, and planned to hike into the lava cliffs in the morning and dig out the pack-rat dropping in the cave where I found the pottery shards.

Recalled that I was nauseated and ill when I was first on the Sonora Desert years before. I blamed the diarrhea and upset on cactus juice then. Could it have been general inability to quickly adjust to heat and exertion?

I chose to live from what the land itself would provide, a drastic break from the supermarket world of instant food and shelter. Besides trying to capture something of the world in which my ancestors lived for more than a million years, I expected something like shock-therapy. If I understand the theory correctly, one is removed from past and future concerns by being thrust into the present. Such an experience brings a gain of new perspective. Rebirth, in the language of many religions, is an expression of this human experience.

Rebirth is more literal than many suspect. The Yucca Moth appears to be a different creature than the red grub which shared the seeds of the Banana Yucca with me at lunch, yet the grub and the moth are the same animal. From its chrysalis, the Swallowtail butterfly, waving its wings on my knee, has been reborn at least once. The butterfly of the human spirit needs to be born again and again.

July 19: "And God called the firmament Heaven. And the evening and the morning were the second day."

It is good to feel fine after last night. I have decided the cause of illness was overexertion, too long in the hot, bright sun, with black lava returning the heat. I'm also sunburned, even though pretty well tanned to begin with. Too much water is also a problem in spite of advice to the contrary by those who write about desert travel. I'll boil some Yucca baccata fruit, then look for meat. Lizards, squirrels, snakes, etc., watch out!

Spent most of the morning collecting a petroglyph which had fallen from a cliff in the canyon—could not get the Jeep closer than half a mile. Temperature in the shade I estimate as over 120 degrees. Back in the shade of a Catclaw, (*Acacia greggi*), I was sick in the wash. Too much exertion in too much heat. Brewed some desert tea, (*E. nevadensis*), great stuff! A little puckery like strong black tea, but not bitter—a good thirst quencher. After resting, I took emergency water and camera and headed for the cave in the lava cliff. Scratched out pottery and a reed arrow shaft, then headed back to the Jeep, as it was over two miles and the heat was getting to me. Decided that I had better camp on higher ground to fight illness which returned, so drove back to my original camping area in the desert hills.

Made a stew of Yucca baccata fruit, Catclaw beans, bullsnake, and lizard. Ate little, and tried to rest, but I am not a well man as these internal rumblings keep reminding me. To combat diarrhea, I shall brew some desert tea—then the starry sky, and sleep.

[This was not my first sojourn like this into the desert. Part of my reason for this journey dates back to an earlier experience. These are my recollections of the time I spent on the Sonoran Desert south of Phoenix, Arizona.

I was seventeen years old and brash enough to tell friends that anyone could live on the desert so long as he knew it and was ingenious. The Papago and Pima Indians managed fairly well.

I am not certain of the month of the year, but it was summer, as school was out and the desert sweltering during the day and not too cool for sleeping comfortably at night without extra clothing. I wore the usual cotton shirt, blue jeans, socks, and shoes. My only tool was a pocket knife. I remember the difficulty removing the top of a barrel cactus, as the blade was too short to cut deep enough without puncturing my hand with the spines. I apparently had some string with me, for I recall tying the knife to a Saguaro stick to macerate the pulp. There was plenty of moisture in the pulp but it tasted green and slightly bitter, not too pleasant. It came back up that night, and by early morning I was sick at both ends. I blamed it on the cactus water but assumed I would develop a tolerance for it.]

July 20: "And the earth brought forth grass and herb yielding seed after his kind, and the tree yielding fruit, whose seed was in itself, after his kind: and God saw that it was good. And the evening and the morning were the third day."

Feel good, think I'll survive! Even the stew tastes better this morning. I shall see about making tools for taking something other than a snake or lizards.

Gathered green fruit of the large Prickly Pear, (*Opuntia engelmanni*). Found the green Tunas need to be boiled to be tasty. The base of the center stalk of the Yucca baccata makes good eating when cooked, and the seeds of its fruit roast into tasty morsels. The fruit of the Hedgehog cactus, (*Echinocereus engelmanni*), is like a strawberry in flavor and color, with the seeds on the inside. However, the birds and squirrels have made their fruit scarce.

Finally found a suitable material for arrows. It is the newer shoots growing in the inner part of a canyon shrub. I think it is a Silktassel, (*Garrya flavenscens, Var. padilla*), growing in a wash above my camp. The grain is long, and when skinned with a piece of chert, can be straightened when fresh cut. It dries light and holds its shape.

Besides chert, used a piece of glass picked up on the roadside. It makes good knives, scrapers, and points for arrows. With a little practice I have become adept at fashioning sharp tools. With Yucca fibers for cord, and Pinon pitch for glue, possibilities in tool making are unlimited!

My Juniper wood bow did not work out as the wood was too brittle for the pull I wanted, and am working on a bow of Live Oak which should work out fine.

Made myself a pair of Yucca sandals for camp wear, to save my canvas shoes which are about gone. With Yucca baccata alone, a person could not only survive, but thrive here!

[I remember on my earlier trip trying to start a fire. I had no matches with me. Using wood from a shrub, possibly a Mesquite or Palo Verde, I worked the plow method of ancient man on a saguaro stick. I could get it smoking, but developing a spark was another matter. I recall weeping with fatigue and exasperation after being unable to start a fire for two days.

After many tries with a throwing stick, I killed a cottontail rabbit. That evening I also blew a glow into a flame. It was a great meal; rabbit, baked Prickly Pear, and a couple of well done lizards. The rabbit was carefully rationed and I cut the meat into strips for drying in the desert sun.

I remember being concerned about salt. We were cautioned to use it in the hot weather. I found a Saltcedar, (Tamarix), growing in a wash, and in sucking the needle-like leaves found a source of saltiness, which I later used to salt lizard and rabbit. Besides these animals, I ate snake, ground squirrel, tortoise, and Chuckwalla. Although Chuckwalla is a lizard, its large size and tastiness put it in a class by itself. Night Hawk eggs were a treat. I tried to snare or hit a quail without success. My staple food was cactus.]

July 21: "And God made two great lights: the greater light to rule the day, and the lesser light to rule the night: He made the stars also. And God set them in the firmament of the heaven to give light upon the earth. And to rule over the day and over the night, and to divide the light from the darkness: and God saw it was good. And the evening and the morning were the fourth day."

The Juniper branches sweep into the stars like black flames and the sagebrush are puffs of white smoke in the moonlight. Ribbons of Juniper bark hang down through the trees like Spanish Moss, and the sharp spikes of Yucca contrast with the oriental outline of a Pinon tree's silhouettes against the sky. I lie in beauty.

Sunrise! Purple mountain ranges—singing yellows, reds, and orange fill the East before the great golden ball pulls up from the horizon. A dove calls from across the draw and the Pinon smoke from my breakfast fire is blue and sweet to smell.

I'll have some broiled Chuckwalla with my desert tea before taking my throwing stick to see if I can collect the cottontail which I saw yesterday afternoon. I can use the rabbit's skin and tendons for a bow cord, and the meat will make jerky. It is a wonderful morning to do other things than push this pen.

Took a cottontail with my throwing stick. I shall use the meat to advantage by making jerky of most—the skin was so tender it came apart in trying to use a chert knife for skinning—will be no good for bow cord. The rabbit is so tender and young that it is not good for much other than food.

It is muggy and the gnats are a nuisance in my ears. Great piles of clouds are stacking up above Table Mountain, but I do not think it will rain—will climb Table Mountain tomorrow. Need feathers for arrows. Prepared an excellent dish with Yucca fruit and fat from the cottontail—flavor like cheese and squash dish my wife once made. The first star is out—the crickets have begun their song and a coyote joins them in the distance. I shall again lie down in beauty.

[Except for the first two or three days when I was ill, my recollection of the week on the Sonora Desert as a teenager was an outstanding experience of my life.

I shall always remember awakening in the shelter of granite rocks to see the distant mountains turn from purple to rose and then have the blazing, golden sun light the world to the song of a canyon wren as if it were the first day.

The nights were the most glorious of all nights I have known, with sparks from my fire glittering toward the stars. I have watched the stars move across the deep dark many times since, as I shall tonight, here on the Mojave. But, that fire on another desert was brought into being by my toil and I was young and life sang to me with the expectations of youth.]

July 22: "And God blessed them, saying be fruitful and multiply, and fill the waters in the seas, and let the fowl multiply on the earth. And the evening and the morning were the fifth day."

I now have feathers for arrows, as a good (lucky) throw with my throwing stick provided hawk feathers. If food were a problem, I would try the hawk for meat. The red-tailed hawk perched on a dead Pinon near my campsite and watched me with curiosity. I was tempted not to throw at him, he was so beautiful and generally unafraid, but I needed feathers.

Feathered the arrows, using Yucca fiber and melting Pinon pitch for glue. My arrowheads are made from chert and glass. I shall complete my bow when I come back from mountain climbing.

Saw my first desert bighorn mountain sheep this trip. There were many petroglyphs of them in the lava canyon to the south. The sheep were a long distance from me, but there was no mistaking the great horns.

Made a second pair of Yucca sandals to save my canvas shoes. After the first pair I made, these are more serviceable and amazingly durable. Except for a lack of callus between my toes where the strap goes, they are easy to wear. I have the knack of weaving them quickly now. I can also turn out a good arrowhead rapidly with the piece of deer antler I found.

Completed my bow after supper of Chuckwalla stew. Delicious.

It is a good bow. The Juniper one broke so shall make a prayer of the Juniper wood and feathers of the golden eyed hawk not used for arrows. I now understand something of the meaning of a prayerstick, so common among the Southwestern Indians.

Cannot find a suitable material for a strong bowstring, so shall use a piece of nylon cord I had in the Jeep.

It was a long day, climbing over granite boulders, high above the surrounding desert. If it were deer season, and I needed one, I am convinced there would be no problem with my new bow. I sat on a game trail overlook behind a Cliff Rose shrub today, and a handsome young buck stood less than twelve feet from me, trying to fathom the mystery he sensed in my presence. I have discovered that when one becomes a part of the area, other life takes you for granted, and as any good hunter knows, game comes to you.

I passed up two opportunities to take rabbits today, because I have dried meat in camp and my needs are less that I ever expected.

The western sky is red and a Canyon wren's cadence rolls down the slope, and all is music.

As I write this, life sings again on a desert breeze through the Juniper overhead. A great granite dome with its Joshua Trees swells to the West, and as the sky turns yellow and scarlet, my eyes flood.

Am I missing something in my diet? Or did I make a mistake and add some of the vision-producing plant, Datura, to my Yucca and lizard stew? The vision is not away in some distant imagining, however. It is here and now in this place. Wasn't it Martin Buber in *Between Man and Man*, who said, "We expect a theophany of which we know nothing but the place, and the place is called community."

Where is community?

Where one stands in the world, not on it.

July 23: "And God saw everything that he had made, and behold, it was very good. And the evening and the morning were the sixth day."

A curious dove flew into the Juniper above my head this morning and my new bow did the trick—wish I could do as well at a target. No complaints. The dark dove meat was delicious.

It is muggy again and the gnats annoying. It is more fun to roam and seek views, food, and the unexpected than to write. I shall climb Table Mountain today. I've decided to make notes of impressions and observations and use the time at home for writing, so as to save these precious hours for what they are and not squander them pushing this pen.

I tell you
I tell you
I tell you
This world is
Whereless world
In the mouth of the
Nameless God.
Seek Him.

The quiet candle
Flame and
The shattering Thunder
Quake
Both do gently
Lead me to that
Delicate Meeting
Place
And Thee.

So wrote Kaye Dunham in his *Divine Mystery*. This week the quiet night and the baking desert glare led me.

July 24: "And on the seventh day God ended his work which he had made; and he rested on the seventh day from all his work which he had made."

Today I wove baskets of Yucca. I made a quiver for my arrows and basketry for my water container. In my normal pattern, I should feel restless, but am content to sit and look and listen both within as well as without. I find I have nothing to write about, really. This sense of being is a kind of fulfillment not easily come by. I shall savor it.

July 25: "And God blessed the seventh day, and sanctified it: because that in it he had rested from all his work which God created and made."

Today I drive to Granite Mountain for a last night before returning to the world of freeways, clocks, and television. The sun is already high, and I have barely started my move to eliminate any trace of my camp. Thunderheads are piled above the Providence Range, and it will surely storm tonight.

July 26: "While the earth remaineth, seedtime and harvest, and cold and heat, and summer and winter, and day and night shall not cease."

He left the land of images of
images and mirrored selves
and myriad motivate roles
to find the center of simplicity
By day he lived to stay alive
He preyed the red-eyed hawk
as hawk would prey the shrew
He made a tool
and sandals for his feet
By night he lay upon
the still-warm turning earth
and watched the universe expand
He made his peace with nature
and with solitude
to find again the being in himself
beyond cerebral reach
too deep for time
too full for space
He wrote a poem for each of us
And sang it to the mourning in our hearts."
—Sarah Ellen

Eskimo Song

The great world has set me in
    motion.
Set me adrift,
    and I move as a weed in
    the river.

The arch of sky
    and mightiness of storms
      encompass me,
And I am left
      trembling with joy.

A Polar Parable
Of Him Who Sings in the Dawn

Now a certain man did rise with the sun. Even with the birds of the morning did he sing for joy and make sounds like unto hymns of the Old Time Religion and Precious Jewels. Singeth he with great gusto, albeit slightly off key.

And they who riseth not with the sun did grumble abominations that he did sing so in the early morn.

And he did harken unto their words and said unto himself: "Even so, should I be quiet for they smile not in the dawn. Peradventure, they require much sleep and speak not with cheer until the sun is well risen."

Then the man who sang hymns did bite his tongue that it might not sing forth.

And it came to pass that one who arose late spoke unto him: "What aileth thee? Art thou sick that thou singest not in the morning? I wouldst hear thy songs of cheer even as the birds at break-up time."

And another spoke thus: "Yea, has thou a burden on thy heart that thou no longer ariseth with song?"

Then the man who riseth early replied: "Even so, when I sing forth in the morning there are those who speak abominations upon my head and with great lamentation cry, 'Knock it off!'"

Then they said unto him: "Nay, we want not to discourage thee. We like thy cheer in the dawn, albeit the words are a bit hard to take in the early morn."

Howsoever, when the dawn did come again and he sang forth of Sunshine in My Soul Today, they did grumble exceedingly as of old.

When the man of Koviashuvik did ponder this, he thinketh: "It is well that some do sing in the dawn, even hymns that are off key, for it is written in the proverbs of old, 'A merry heart doeth good like medicine: but a broken spirit drieth the bones.'"

Postscript

There is something in traveling beyond the ends of the earth, in living in a different world which men have not discovered, in cutting loose from the bonds of world-wide civilization. Such life holds a joy and exhilaration which most explorers today cannot understand, with their radios and aeroplanes which make the remotest corners of the world just a few days or even hours away in distance. Modern mechanical ingenuity has brought many good things to the world, but in the long list of high values which it has ruined one of the greatest is the value of isolation.

—Robert Marshall

*The view
beyond the cabin.*

August

TODAY THE MOUNTAINS SHOUT with color. Caribou and moose, in their great autumn antlers, step majestically on a golden tundra splashed with crimson kinikinnik. Blueberries are ripe for the taking by jaybirds, ptarmigan and the grizzly bear. Snowy white Dall sheep gaze down from rocky crags where wolves and humans seldom venture.

I shall venture because it is harvest time. Our winter meat will be hung in the cache along with memories of sun, snow flurries and endless vistas. Yet I know the true harvest of the wild cannot be hung in a cache or entombed in the mind.

Although it is as haunting as the cry of a loon, the harvest of my life here is not in memory any more than adventure is in a guidebook. It is something like a rainbow—a relationship of sunlight, water particles, and the viewer. Remove one of the ingredients, or change the relationship, and the rainbow no longer exists.

The harvest of the wild is as intangible as beauty. And yet it is as real as the bonds which tie us to each other and this earth which is our home.

Weather

August is the wettest month of the year. Frequent rainy skies account for the sharp drop in sunshine and temperature. The nights begin to darken rapidly. By the end of the month light snows and occasional freezing temperatures can be expected.

In late August the first bands of caribou begin their migration back over the mountains to the southern slope of the range. They are followed by the ever-present wolves.

On a clear night, the haunting howls of a pack at a fresh kill and the first displays of the northern lights are reminders of the coming cold.

An Arctic Allegory
Of Pictures

On a certain day a plane did land on the lake and it taxied to shore where the man of Koviashuvik and the woman of wisdom dwelt in their small log cabin.

And they put on the coffee pot and invited them who visited to make themselves at home. Thereupon the bush pilot and a youth did pause and relax.

Peradventure, the other passengers paused not but clicked their cameras exceedingly at the snowy peaks and the moose hide drying in the sun by the cache. And they did flash their cameras in the cabin at the woman of wisdom and the man of Koviashuvik.

Then he who probably pays the bill, looked upon his watch saying: "Time is upon us. We must be on our way." And thereupon did he depart for the airplane. Then the youth called out saying: "Gee, nothing have I seen yet!"

Then he who looked at his watch said: "Get thy butt into the plane! You can see the pictures when we get home."

And when they were gone, the man of Koviashuvik did ponder all this and spake thus to the woman of wisdom: "How often it is that those who seek to find themselves in the midst of reality prefer a picture."

Intangible as Beauty—Mysticism

Today, a bush pilot friend who carried a hunter into the mountains was returning to Fairbanks. He glided his float plane down onto the lake and taxied ashore to ask if we had any mail we wanted flown out.

Before he left, he said, "My client left me some apples brought in from the lower forty-eight. Here, have one."

Then the plane lifted off and droned into the distance while I rubbed the ripe, red globe on my sleeve until its shining waxy surface glowed with the attention I gave it.

As silence replaced the sound of the aircraft, I bit into the juice-laden fruit. There was a familiar snap with that first bite, followed by a crackle between the teeth, a flow of the sweet, rich taste around the tongue, and a pungent odor in my nostrils.

In that moment I was nine years old, with the feel of wet grass against my feet, standing in the heat of the day in a deserted homestead orchard in New Mexico. I saw the white faces of Hereford cattle lying and standing in the shade of cottonwood trees, and the feel and taste of that ripe apple into which I'd just bitten.

Even here, on the shore of an arctic mountain lake, the experience of eating an apple can be rich in its variety. I find it interesting how unbidden creative imagining has a way at times of pouring experience and much more into the one word, "apple."

Like beauty, the experience has an intangible quality. Most people have had this kind of experience. Philosophically and religiously it is called mysticism.

∽

As I hiked up through a bronze and gold autumn from the shore, I wondered about this experience called mystic. I am sure it is in everyone's experience in some form or other.

Have you ever walked along with the completely trusting hand of a small child in yours and suddenly felt that you and the youngster were part and parcel of the same lifestream? Or, have you gazed into the sky on a starlit night and felt no vacancy or strangeness between the stars and you? Or, have you dreamed of that full and complete physical, mental, and spiritual love; perhaps found in many degrees, but maybe not, but the vision remains?

If such things have happened for you, you know what I am referring to when I use the term mysticism. Mysticism arises largely as the result of what is felt to be a failure in the more usual ways of seeking an understanding of life and the universe.

∾

Knowledge gained through sense perception and the use of the mind is partial and limited. In some ways it appears not to reveal but to obscure the nature of the universe. There seems no way that our mind and senses can penetrate the real mysteries of life and lead an individual to the heart of reality.

The age-old tradition of mysticism is primarily a method of obtaining knowledge. It arises largely as the result of certain human experiences, such as I had with the apple, and senses in these a way of seeking an understanding of life and its meaning.

Like most philosophies and faiths, mysticism expresses the audacity and unbounded egotism of us humans. For of all living things, human beings appear to be driven by the need to feel all-important, all-powerful, and all-knowing. No other creature demands to know the secrets of the universe, to find cosmic support for its wishes and desires, to be assured that its own individual life is of supreme and unending significance to all creation.

Mysticism seems to operate on a two-fold assumption: First, that the individual yearns for union with the substance of the universe itself; and second, that through such a union, one will obtain a vision of truth that far surpasses anything that can be reached by any other means. A vision of truth, that in peace and joy and power which it brings, will so relate us that we find union with all existence.

A mystic says that real knowledge comes not through sense experience or the use of reason, but through intense experience of the inner life. By means of this inner vision, the mystic is able to apprehend truths not otherwise available. Mysticism asserts that all things are not what they appear to be. It asserts that there is an inner essence or meaning to the universe, and to life, which we fail to grasp by the ordinary methods of approach.

Therefore, the purpose of mysticism is to jar people out of their lethargy, to make them realize that they are missing the greatest joy of life because they do not go beyond the mere surface appearance of things to the heart of reality which those appearances conceal.

Mysticism affirms that there is a unity of reality, that the universe is one and that we can only know reality by merging ourselves within it in the mystic experience.

Our usual tendency, through the use of our minds and our senses, is to chop the world up into bits and label them with words or other symbols, when in truth all reality is one. In the mystic experience, any part of the world about us is somehow inclusive of the total. Therefore, the individual can look either without or within and find the same thing.

Idealists are wrong, say the mystics, when they try to reduce everything to mind. And equally, the materialists are wrong when they try to reduce everything to matter or energy. For in truth, all are ultimately one and the same. For us to label anything mind or matter may be convenient, so far as communication is concerned, but as far as a description of reality, these are only constructs. They are temporary inventions we have created to help us communicate.

In the mystic experience, a person can know the whole of reality by experiencing fully and intimately any small part of it. Thus, Tennyson wrote:

Flower in the crannied wall,
I pluck you out of the crannies,
I hold you here, root and all, in my hand,
Little flower—but if I could understand
What you are, root and all, and all in all,
I should know what God and man is.

To know and to experience something completely is to know the heart of reality. And since it is easier to know that with which we are most intimately connected, that is, our own self, mystics by and large concentrate on an understanding of the inner life and what dwells within.

Mystics also insist that it is not only possible to reach an intuitive knowledge and union with reality but that it is also vitally important. This is because there is no falsity, no mistake, no error when a person in the midst of a mystic experience becomes the whole of reality. So the mystic encourages others to strive for this state within which all things are one and true.

However, there is a problem here. Although a person in the mystic experience apprehends the whole of reality, when she or he comes out of that experience and back into the ordinary world, she or he cannot communicate the findings to others. Although a person may try, a mystic experience cannot be fully communicated by the use of words.

Moreover, this state is also an intellectual, moral, and physical retreat into a kind of existence which is completely other from what we consider that of a normal human being.

By freeing one's self from the bribes of society, the confusions of partial knowledge, and the petty allurements of the senses, the mystic asserts that out of this experience, which is impossible to communicate, you gain a serenity of spirit which is characteristic of what has been called the divine.

Mystics are convinced that they have a kind of knowledge and understanding which others lack, and which, because of that lack, causes them to be unhappy, disturbed, anxious, and fearful. And so I ask myself, what does it mean? What is the role of this mystical temperament and its claim to some kind of ultimate knowledge?

Then high overhead, against a cloudless blue, a wavering vee of Canadian geese send down their faint honking to each other on their way south for the winter. Like the mystics, they seem to have a special knowledge also. Would it be called a mystical temperament?

∽

I am aware that men and women of mystic temper have given much beauty and insight to the world. This has been not only in the fields of art and philosophy, but also in science. Some of our greatest scientists have also been mystics. There is a deeper element in reality than that which we experience on the surface. For this reason we all have a need for periods of withdrawal, when the human spirit can examine itself and the life it is living. In this process the self seeks a deeper understanding of the nature of that which surrounds it, dwells within, and upholds it. We have only begun to penetrate the depths of this spirit within us.

On the other hand, we cannot totally rely only on inner illumination for truth. We must guard against confusing intense feeling with certain knowledge.

We can feel very intense about an idea which is obviously false to the nature of reality. Because a person is possessed by a strong and real emotional state, it does not follow that she or he has an access to the ultimate nature of reality which is denied to other individuals.

❧

Studies of the human psyche have made us aware that in the mystical experience the individual is experiencing with emotional intensity what in most cases he or she already knows. The intellectual content which is given to this experience is the same which was taken into the experience. In other words, in the mystical experience an individual discovers what was sought. Then he or she proclaims it as the inner secret of reality. But more than this, it is then assumed as proof that the human spirit is the same as that of the universe.

For example, when the Hindu mystic returns from his mystic state he expresses the meaning of it in terms of Brahma and his Hindu religion. The Christian mystic brings back to us a revelation of the creator we find described in the Bible. Saint Francis, when he had his great mystical experience, produced the nail marks, or stigmata of Christ on his body. He did not reproduce anything which would relate him to the traditions of Buddhism, the Muslims, or any other religious tradition. He returned from his experience with Christian truths that he already held and believed before he went into his trance.

So no matter how nebulous, or incapable of description, the intellectual content of the mystic experience always corresponds in the end to his or her previous convictions.

❧

I am aware that there are, in the experience of most of us, those moments when we are suddenly aware of what is felt to be new insight. Sometimes our greatest discoveries are made in the flash of a moment when we have become jaded from rational analysis and experimental investigation. I am also aware that the ideas and beliefs revealed by such intuitions are the fruit of previous experience and are hypotheses to be tested by further experience. For the truth of any conception or idea is not the intensity of the feeling which it induces but its correspondence to the facts of existence.

Each of us yearns to identify with the larger life of the universe. No person is truly content to live a life completely to one's self and unrelated to some larger meaning. This yearning or hunger for a larger frame of reference is fed and stimulated by many experiences: the beauty of a scene of nature, the chords of harmony in a great work of music, the creativity of the human mind when it produces a new idea or work of art. It is expressed especially in the experience of creativity when a person brings into being something which is transformed, reformed out of the old, and which gives a finer expression to the inner spirit.

Even in as simple an experience as the eating of an apple.

No Secret

Today I learned again
    of water earth and air and fire.
I know,
    with ancient Greeks, the Eskimos
    and Australian bushmen
That these are the source of life
    and without them
    we shall perish
    from the earth.

Not just the flow of our blood
    The substance of our bones
    The oxidizer of our food
    And the spark which gives life,
    They are life itself.
What is the self,
    but sound of running water
    silence of the earth
    breath of air
    and warmth of fire.
So share with me
    this fire
    this water
    this air
    and this earth.

A Polar Parable
Of Giving Advice

In the days of the midnight sun, the man of Koviashuvik did labor to build a new cache wherein meat and supplies might be safe from beasts of the wilderness; even the great grizzly bear, wolf, and wolverine, likewise the vole and tiny shrew.

Swingeth he his axe, and peeleth he the bark from trees that he might raise the heavy poles thereupon to build the cache.

And he did work to make a platform six cubits high and four cubits wide thereupon to construct his cache from the trees of the forest.

And while he labored thus, there visited an aircraft with diverse fishermen who did tarry to give advice. And one said, "Why hast thou not a chainsaw?"

And another said, "Thou needest a fork-lift, albeit with a block and tackle thou couldst with ease lift the logs."

And another said, "Why dost thou not do thus and so?"

Even so, their counsel was of small worth to him that labored. Then one did step forward, and speaking little did labor mightily so that the cache was soon prepared.

The man of Koviashuvik did ponder these things and made this proverb: "If thou wouldst give good advice to him who lifteth a log, pick up the other end."

Postscript

Genuine mental health would involve a way of life in which one's identification with the ego is playful and tentative rather than absolute and mandatory, while the concern with material possessions is pragmatic rather than obsessive. Such a way of being would be characterized by an affirmative attitude toward life, an emphasis on the present moment, and a deep awareness of the spiritual dimension of existence.

—Fritjof Capra

Jeff Whaley photo

Time for filling the cache
before winter.

September

NORTH OF THE ARCTIC CIRCLE there is a feeling of restlessness at this turn of the season. I sense this unease as something to resist if I am to spend the winter here. There is a bite of cold in the air which drifts down the mountain slopes. I wonder if it is the first frosts which produce this restlessness?

This feeling of unease is familiar. I felt it last spring when the ya-honk of high flying geese awakened me on their way north.

Did I again hear them on their way south? Or is the call within me?

I've discovered that the call which lifts loons and gulls against the sky, and sends the arctic tern 11,000 miles south across the globe, is also my call. Some of us still respond to ancient cycles deep within that mysterious matrix which composes our bodies. Thus, I too would follow the southern sun as the earth tips toward the cold of arctic night.

But not the Eskimo. They take delight in shorter days and stars not seen in arctic summer. There is no southward pull for them. They look with anticipation to the cold which thickens pelts. They delight in snow which covers brush and tussocks, making thaw-ponds potential trails for sleds and snowmachines. Their restlessness is of a different kind.

The giant moose are also restless because this is the season of rut and their hormones cannot be denied at this autumn turn of the year.

North of the Arctic Circle this turn invokes such meaning and drama that, if it were not for my sense of reason, I feel I could flap my wings and with a great ya-honk follow the birds.

Instead, I shall take my restlessness across the lake with my camera—where, through my field glasses, I have seen the great white antlers of a moose.

Weather

By September the rainy season is over and temperatures show a steady lowering. Snow has replaced rain by the end of the month. Nighttime temperatures are frequently well below freezing. The aurora is visible on clear nights and snow remains on the mountain tops and hills.

Migratory waterfowl have flown south, leaving only a few ducks and loons on the still open water of the larger lakes. Ice forms along the shore. Freeze-up will soon begin.

Caribou and moose finish polishing their antlers and lake trout complete spawning on the rocky shoals. Ptarmigan and ermine, along with snowshoe hares, have turned white and the crimson lingonberries are ripe for picking.

An Arctic Allegory
Of Approaching a Moose

Now it came to pass that the man of Koviashuvik did sneak up on a bull moose albeit to take his picture.

And it was so that the moose saw him not, for the bull moose was observing a cow moose making moose eyes from where she stood in the marshy shallows.

Then did the man of Koviashuvik slip through the brush even as a lynx creepeth upon the snowshoe hare. And the bull moose saw him not, peradventure this moose had eyes only for her who stood in the water.

And the man of Koviashuvik did raise his camera, Howsoever, he clicked it not, as a strange noise did sound behind him.

Then did he turn to see another bull moose pacing toward him. Yea, with loud snorts did it come as it flung forth tundra it had torn up with its mighty antlers!

Then the man of Koviashuvik did scramble up a spruce tree lest the moose flingeth him also. Even so the moose did strike the tree a mighty blow.

And time did pass and the moose and all the great beasts tramped back into the timber leaving the man of Koviashuvik up a tree.

Then thinketh the man of Koviashuvik: "So it has always been. He who gives too much attention ahead finds himself vulnerable from behind."

Tuktuwak: Giant Of The North

As quietly as possible, I moved through the brushy willows among scattered white spruce trees. I did not want to spook the great bull moose. He was standing knee deep in water a short distance from the lake shore.

His attention was focused on two female moose feeding in the shallows several hundred feet away. When a dry twig broke beneath my step, he turned his head toward me.

I froze, motionless.

The huge animal's polished antlers were white in the morning sunlight. They spread like great wings on either side of his massive head and neck as he peered intently toward the brushy shore to see what had distracted him.

This was the largest moose I had seen in the Brooks Range. At break-up I had watched him browse on new, green willow shoots in the swale below our cabin. At midsummer, while his antlers were still in the velvet, I had been able to estimate his height by comparison with a dead spruce tree next to which he had stood. He was over seven feet tall at the shoulder.

Except for the grey-gold of the shoulder hump, his coat was almost black. He had stayed in the vicinity of our lake feeding on water plants in the shallow bays. On one occasion, when a family of wolves had frightened him into the lake, I had filmed him swimming in open water toward the opposite shore.

Now, at breeding season, he had rubbed the velvet from his antlers. They shone, polished by frequent attacks on small trees, willows, and tussocks.

For the past two weeks he had stopped browsing on the sedges and tender willows. His belligerence, in this period of rut, expressed itself in uprooting alders and small trees. In one clump of white spruce, he had torn a twelve-foot-tall tree out of the tundra by its roots. In an area nearby, other great patches of tundra had been plowed up by the palmate shovels of his antlers.

As his attention turned back to the two cows, he gave a series of loud, deep, grunting "ughs," while standing motionless in the shallow water.

With the low morning sun shining directly into my camera, I continued along the shore toward the cows behind a screen of alders and scrub willow. I hoped to be able to film the courtship of these largest deer on the North American continent.

After reaching an advantageous position, I unslung my rifle, a wilderness insurance policy where grizzly bear are common. Leaning the gun against a small spruce tree, I readied the camera and listened to the measured grunts of the bull moose as he moved slowly through the shallows toward the cows.

Through an opening in the trees I had a clear view of the females. The light was good and the bull would also soon appear unobstructed by willow or alder.

෴

Unlike the majestic bulls, who, with their great antlers and regal stance, seem designed for this great land, the cow moose appears to be an afterthought. Her flexible, overhanging nose at the end of a long face is far from balanced by her mule-like ears.

One of the cows raised her head while chewing rhythmically on a clump of green water plants. Then, stepping high, she moved into shallower water.

I was struck by how disproportionate her neck and long legs seemed in relation to the bulk of her huge, tailless body. But then I thought, long legs are just what is needed for wading in soft muskeg and silt-bottomed ponds and lakes. Long legs are particularly handy for stepping over sedge tussocks and through deep snows. With her long neck, she can reach high for browsing, and her large ears can catch the faintest sound. Not a bad design at that, I thought. Even the bull, after shedding his mighty antlers, has an appearance in the winter time much like a large moose cow.

∾

I was so engrossed in observing the three moose in the water that I did not hear a sound behind me until a sudden crash of breaking branches spun me around. There was another bull moose, no more than fifty feet away, hooking his great palmate rack through dry willows.

As I faced him, he pawed the turf with a foreleg. Then, lowering his head, he thrust an antler into a tussock and flung a chunk of tundra into the air.

I looked for the nearest tree large enough and tall enough to take me out of reach. They were all much too small!

I know that I set the camera down quickly and as quickly reached for my rifle. However, my actions seemed as methodical and deliberate as slow motion.

The giant moose appeared to fill two-thirds of the space in front of me as he made deep gruff sounds and twisted his huge rack from side to side. It was one of those uncompromising moments that required immediate action. But even while in motion, my mind took in details and considered possibilities.

◡

During rut, bull moose are not only irritable, fighting with each other, but are also unpredictable. Although they will usually run from a human being, there are graves in Alaska which attest that this is not always so. I was not only between this bull and the cows, but the other bull moose was still grunting his maleness in the shallows behind me. It must have seemed to the moose I was facing that the sounds had come from me!

Except in the mating season, moose tend to be silent. My attention had originally been caught by the wailing bawl of one of the cows. The sound had carried on the wind across the water of the lake to my cabin. Spotting the two cows and the big bull through field glasses, I had taken camera and rifle and rowed to a hidden point of land near their rendezvous. With the bull's attention focused on the cows, I had found it easy to make a close approach through the brushy alders, willows, and spruce trees. Because of this same diversion, I now found myself facing this other large bull only a few yards away. I knew I had to act.

From my hip, I fired the rifle over his head and quickly thrust another cartridge into the breech as I threw the gun to my shoulder.

With the loud report of the rifle, he stopped, swung himself around, defecating as he paced off through the high willows. He stopped once and looked back at me.

Then, with the loud splashing in the shallows, made by the other moose as they fled, he also continued on and paced quickly out of sight.

∾

The moose of the Brooks Range are the largest wild animals on the continent. A prime bull can weigh from 1,500 to 2,000 pounds or more. Their antlers can spread from six to seven feet. These Alaskan moose are considerably larger than those to the south, as well as those in the northeastern United States and Canada.

The Eskimo call him Tuktuwak, giant deer.

To dress a bull for winter meat and haul it to the cache is an all-day task. It is easy to understand why the Nunamiut Eskimos and Athapaskan Indians of the foothills of the range, when hunting, would move their camp to the vicinity of a downed moose rather than try to haul it to their present campsite.

After mating season, the bulls shed their antlers. And in late October or early November, along with the cows, they seek the sheltered valleys of the range where willows project above the snow, providing winter feed.

Willow is the staple diet of moose in the Brooks Range. The frozen twigs and dead leaves appear to have all the necessary nourishment to adequately supply their needs during the long winter of subzero temperatures.

Calves are born at break-up time, in late May or early June. Unlike most members of the deer family, their coats are not spotted. Their cinnamon-brown color turns dark during the summer. By autumn the calves are as dark as their mothers.

The calf stays with its mother through the first winter. But by calving time in the spring, it will have been abandoned to make its own way.

When the willows have turned golden in autumn and the great bulls are rubbing the velvet from their antlers, the yearlings will already weigh half a ton.

Based upon remains dug from the permafrost, ancestors of the Alaskan moose were even larger than today's great bulls. They roamed the Brooks Range during the Pleistocene. This is their ancestral home.

As I rowed back across the lake, recounting the experience I had just had, I felt no chagrin at not getting the film I had hoped for. I had been an intruder, a two-legged voyeur. But for a few minutes I had known, in a most intimate way, what it was like to participate in the life of Tuktuwak, the giant of the north.

Assertion

Beginnings start
    where ends leave.
Between the two,
    creation,
    which is here
    and now.
It is now
    that we are,
    now
    that we act
    now that we live.

A Polar Parable
Of Ferocious Animals

It came to pass that it stormed mightily. The man of Koviashuvik and diverse guides and hunters were weathered in at an airfield in the far north where bush planes flew into the wilderness. Thus it also came to pass that those who gathered in the lodge did sit and tell each other tales of great beasts that had been encountered.

Spoke they of the charge of the rhinoceros, the tramp of the elephant, and the stealth of the panther; also of the great grizzly bear that even here they did come to hunt. And each did speak of a ferocious animal that had been met.

While sitting there, the man of Koviashuvik did listen to them who lieth not, yet avoided the truth, before he too spoke unto the multitude, saying: "The most ferocious animal liveth at Koviashuvik wherein I dwell with the woman of wisdom. He who protecteth not himself shall suffer mightily. Yea, even may he die."

Silence then fell upon the gathering for they knew the man of Koviashuvik dwelt deep on the wilderness of the far north and spoke with knowledge.

Then one did open his mouth, saying: "Wouldst thou tell us the name of this beast, peradventure we might protect ourselves?"

And the man of Koviashuvik sayeth: "Thou knowest her well. She is called the mosquito!"

Then did they all nod their heads and murmur: "It is so."

Postscript

Politicians at international forums may reiterate a thousand times that the basis of the new world order must be universal respect for human rights, but it will mean nothing as long as this imperative does not derive from the respect of the miracle of being, the miracle of the universe, the miracle of nature, the miracle of our own existence.

—Vaclav Havel

*Tracks in the
early winter snow.*

October

TODAY MARKS THE BEGINNING of freeze-up. Hour by hour the freezing can actually be seen on the lake. A light dusting of white from falling snow marks the ice. This is in contrast to dark, open, water channels that branch out across the surface like a somewhat confused interconnecting web.

An experience which is a daily delight here north of the Arctic Circle is seeing the old in a new way. The moon is an example. When the earth's northern axis turns away from the sun, the moon appears to stay in its same orbit around the earth. Tonight it never dropped below the horizon. It returned to the north where it was first seen last night. There it touched the horizon of jagged peaks before swinging up across the sky again. Its lowest dip is the axis of the earth, true north.

People have been aware of the moon's orbit since ancient times. Tonight I saw the way I used to see as a child. One of the delights of the wild is to find the lost child again.

I also found the lost child in Polaris. The north star is so nearly overhead at this latitude that there is no question that I am standing near the top of the world!

And then there are the northern lights. Before moving into this arctic wilderness, I was aware that the aurora could be bright and colorful with iridescent reds, yellows, greens, and blues. But tonight the motion is a great spirit dance, flashing from horizon to horizon across the high dome of the universe. It makes music I never suspected.

Rationally, I know it is not possible to hear the northern lights, but they do sing. I am not sure it was with ears or something within responding to the earth's magnetism, but I heard.

And there is the cold. It too has its delights, makes its songs. Tonight, outside our cabin window, the top of the mercury line on the Fahrenheit thermometer has dropped to twenty degrees below the zero mark.

The lake now sings in a deep bass, like the rumbling of a great stomach as ice freezes thicker, making seams snap and growl from shore to shore.

The sky and lake are alive as they adjust for winter. Alive, as one is alive who sees the world as for the first time, or sees the old in a new way.

Weather

Winter begins in earnest in October with temperatures dropping well below freezing.

Late one October, I recorded a temperature of thirty degrees below zero.

Six to ten inches of snow can be expected. Lakes and rivers become frozen and sunshine decreases rapidly.

This is the month of hibernation for squirrels and bears. The migratory birds have all gone and only the voices of ravens, jays, and chickadees are heard.

Nights are longer than days and at noon the sun skirts the tops of mountains in a pale blue southern sky.

An Arctic Allegory
Of Prayer and the Selling of Chariots

It came to pass that the man of Koviashuvik needed not his chariot since the wilderness hath no roads. And thus it was that in a certain city of the far north he did bargain with one who buyeth and selleth used chariots for that which passes as gold.

And it also came to pass that he who dealt in used chariots had of late got religion, and spake he of being saved. And he who had been saved did inquire of the man of Koviashuvik therewith if he also hath been converted?

The man of Koviashuvik, having been accosted aforetimes by those who would have him saved, said, "Yea, even so! More years than two score have I been ordained and serve the church of my fathers."

Then spake he even more, of the seminary of theology where he had been a professor, thinking: "This mayest assure him who hath been saved." For the man of Koviashuvik liked not the gleam in eye of the buyer and seller of chariots.

Howsoever, the man who selleth chariots wouldst not be put off, and he said: "Even so I work in the fields of the lost! Kneel thee down with me and I shall offer prayers that the will of the Lord may be manifest."

Then thinketh the man of Koviashuvik: " 'Tis a strange place for kneeling." But even so did he kneel down. On the thick carpet of the salesroom did he bend his knee, for great was his need to sell and he wanted not to offend him who would buy his chariot.

With bended knee on a thick padded rug, he who buyeth and selleth did pray many words. Spake he of widows and the fatherless. Spake he also of giving and receiving, but even more so, of the blessings of poverty did he make many words.

And while he spake thus of poverty, even so did light flash on his bracelet of nuggets of fine gold that held his watch set with bright jewels. Even the great diamond in his ring did flash in the eye of the man of Koviashuvik.

Then he of long prayer finally rose, saying: "Let us get down to the business of thy chariot. Peradventure, you realize not that the bottom has dropped out of the market for used chariots. It is therefore a small sum that I can pay thee. Albeit, praise the Lord, I can offer thee something!"

Then the man of Koviashuvik, knowing that he had been had, spake thus: "Whatever thou offerest, that shall I take. The chariot must be sold."

Then pondereth the man of Koviashuvik upon his return to the wilderness:"The voice of truth is seldom hidden, for that which flasheth in the eye doth speak more truly than ardent prayer."

Old in a New Way

Among the letters brought in by the bush plane was one from a scientist friend including an Associated Press clipping from Los Angeles headlined **Detection of Neutrinos Supports Theory on Stars.** The article read:

> A device deep beneath the Alps apparently has detected tiny particles emitted by an exploding star, unprecedented evidence that dying stars are reborn as neutron stars or black holes, scientists said Thursday.
>
> If confirmed by other observers, the discovery made at Mont Blanc by Italian and Russian physicists also would be the first time the minuscule particles called neutrinos have been linked to a source outside our solar system, U.S. researchers said.

This clipping with the word "neutrino" touched off a reminiscence of the time I was with the Office of Scientific Research and Development in New Mexico during World War II.

Getting up from my comfortable seat in front of the Yukon Stove, I took the *New College Edition of the American Heritage Dictionary* from its spruce board shelf and looked up the word, neutrino. It was defined as, "Either of two massless electrically neutral, stable subatomic particles in the lepton family." Then there was this quotation: "Neutrinos zip through the earth as if it weren't there...the great problem with studying neutrinos is catching them in the first place."

When I first heard of the neutrino it did not exist. I remember a conversation I had with a colleague shortly after the explosion of the first atomic bomb at Alamagordo.

"What is this neutrino you mentioned? Who discovered it?"

"Nobody discovered it. We invented it."

"What for?"

"Well, without it the atom is lopsided. We wanted to balance the cosmic books."

"OK, but are you an accountant? Why so eager to balance?"

"We are trying to hold on to the principle of the conservation of energy. You know, nothing is ever lost or created, just changed. But it is getting difficult."

"Is that so? What difference would it make if you gave up the principle of the conservation of energy?"

"Oh, that couldn't happen. We would be living in a world where anything could happen. Do you believe in miracles?"

∽

The existence of the neutrino has since been verified. It does exist. The principle of the conservation of energy, that nothing is ever really lost from the world, is still the key conception which nourished in many the intoxicating hope of reducing the whole bewildering cosmos to some form of understandable natural law.

Albert Einstein once said that "the supreme task of the physicist is to arrive at those universal, elementary laws from which the cosmos can be built up by pure deduction."

His attempt to formulate a unified field theory never wavered. He died, leaving a new set of alleged universal equations for the consideration of posterity. Among the last things he said when confronted with the new quantum physics was, "I cannot believe that God throws dice with men."

∽

This hope to express at some point the cosmic plan in one master formula, intelligible to all who have brains enough to understand it, seems to make obvious why the conservation of energy principle is just about the last thing our scientists wish to relinquish.

When I was at Los Alamos during World War II, no less an authority than J. Robert Oppenheimer raised the question in a way that was disturbing for many of us young scientists when he asked, "Will this world, with its variety, its un-understood numbers, ever yield to an ordered description, simple and necessary?"

His question came back as I stepped outside the cabin to relieve myself and watched the northern lights curtain in iridescent gyrations above the crags across the frozen lake.

Is there really free will? I asked myself.

∾

This old question, I had once debated for hours, is easy to resolve in this wilderness context. I can state my position very simply. Like William James, my first act of free will is to affirm free will. Here, in this northern vastness, the old arguments about free will versus determinism seem naive, for they fail to take into account the acting person.

The way a person defines his or her situation constitutes its reality. Choice is a paramount fact of personal life. We must constantly choose and act; therefore, accept responsibility for our decisions.

Modern psychology, in spite of its many deterministic tendencies, confirms certain conditions of relative freedom for the individual. One of the most important of these is self insight. We consider a person freer if she or he understands himself better. By this I mean that she or he is in a better position to weigh inclinations, comprehend possibilities and limitations, and pursue a self-chosen course of action. This self knowledge is a doorway to freedom. It is a relative freedom to be sure, since no freedom is absolute, but self insight is a freedom.

∾

Western perspectives have been plagued through the centuries by the goodness/badness theory of human nature: people do good because there is good in them; they do evil because there is evil in them. In this framework, the task of religion is not freedom, but the compelling of people to stop being bad and become good. The dominance of this theory helps explain why so many religious perspectives are authoritarian.

We now know that most so-called "bad behavior" is the product of frustration, warped reasoning, sick emotions, and immature ways of solving problems. In the solitude of this mountain fastness it would appear that the proper role of religion is to keep underlining, with emotional intensity, the freedom we have to move toward a mature, fuller living. Tonight I find it conceivable that as time goes on it will become easier to believe in a world where God enjoys throwing dice with us than one which someone can wrap up in a unified field theory.

But is this not just a temporary difference of opinion among experts? Will it not inevitably be decided one day by some new discovery which will tip the balance in favor of one of the two views?

For me the confusion is not due to any absence of facts, but to the presence of two different kinds of facts.

The late English physicist and astronomer, Arthur Stanley Eddington, put it this way: "Like most people, I suppose, I think it incredible that the wider scheme of nature, which includes life and consciousness, can be completely predetermined: yet I have been unable to form a satisfactory conception of any kind of law or causal sequence which shall be other than deterministic."

The French philosopher Henri Bergson proclaimed his belief that the biologically late developing, rational intellect is indeed a marvelous tool for solving human problems in the physical world, but totally unable to grasp the inward flow which is the heart of reality. We are conscious of these two types of experience in which one of them responds wonderfully to observation and logic, particularly mathematical logic. This experience points to an intelligible world. The other has its own laws, essentially freedom and spontaneity, and cannot be systematized in the same way.

Since both of these systems are genuine, both can claim validity. I find little difficulty in leaping from one to the other even though they point to radically different worlds. As long as they remain separate, however, they prevent any final conclusion as to the nature of reality.

From this perspective, I observed that people tend to break up into two schools of opinion about the universe and life. And I have concluded that it is not a matter of unequal knowledge or intellectual power, but of temperament, of an inner commitment or need. Thus, an Albert Einstein wanted, even needed, a closed cosmos. He spent his life trying to demonstrate its existence. An unbalanced atom was to him not only repugnant, but in a religious sense, blasphemous.

On the other hand, a person like Bergson or Eddington instinctively leaned toward an open-ended universe and proceeded to marshal weighty reasons why it had to be so.

∞

Alfred North Whitehead said: Philosophy begins in wonder, and at the end, when philosophy has done its best, the wonder remains.

It seems to me that I can generally classify those who wonder in two ways. First are those who have a distaste for the open, endless, wild blue yonder, who love limits and are uncomfortable with the uncircumscribable, the indeterminate, or formless. On the other hand, there are those who resent restrictions and aspire to what is open, endless, and unexpected.

Or, to say it another way, there are those who, looking at the sky of stars, see and admire the army of unalterable law. Then there are others who immediately start dreaming of endless galaxies and wonderlands where all things may be different.

I think of the Spinoza or Einstein type of thinkers who, even when they merely observe the world, instinctively seem to reach for the natural law beneath all phenomena and soon discover a closed cosmos. And by contrast, the others who read with delight any criticisms of scientific dogmatism and readily convince themselves that the uniformity which others discover in nature is a projection from within the observer and not inherent in the things themselves.

Both of these attitudes we can find within ourselves. But I must admit that as long as I can recall, I have sought the open universe. Any mountain range, canyon, or cave was exciting, especially if one might meet a wild animal like a wolverine or rattlesnake. But a mountain range, canyon, or cavern that one could never explore completely was best. I find that I respond in the same way to ideas and philosophies. I am a lover of the wild. And wildness, as defined by the zoologist N.J. Berril is essentially this quality of unpredictability that defies control.

In the literary field, this would make me a romantic rather than a classical type. Knowing that apples fall regularly to the ground is fine if you want apples. But how much more exciting it would be if every now and then an apple would go sailing off into the sky! A unified field theory would be a unique scientific achievement. But to some it would be a painful shrinkage of the area of surprise and anticipation.

∽

Some time ago I discovered a kindred spirit in an Indian Brahmin who lived in the eleventh century. His name was Nimbarka. When Nimbarka postulated Brahma (what we would call Creator, or God, in western terms) as eternally perfect, satisfied, and blissful, he faced a baffling question: Why then should he have created anything?

Nimbarka answered his question with the very unusual, but to me attractive doctrine of Lilivada: Creation for fun or play.

Fun or play in this sense is both spontaneous and purposeless. I find this an intriguing idea which may be shocking to some. But of all the doctrines foisted upon us, it is as believable as most, particularly in contrast to the dictum that to be a true Christian one must renounce the self and come to God with a contrite and broken spirit.

Whether one is a believer in the open universe, or believes that it is ultimately definable, the essence of life is spontaneity.

Today those opponents of closed systems are no longer seen as enemies of science or obscurantists. They have become a part of science itself. They welcome demonstrable discoveries and delight in fruitful theories. But they instinctively question any too-positive assertion or dogma. In the backs of their minds is the suspicion, clearly expressed by Santayana, that all alleged knowledge of matters of fact is faith, and an existing world, whatever form it may take, is intrinsically a questionable and arbitrary thing.

I was reminded of this when the late astronomer Harlow Shapely made the flat statement to a group of us some years ago that "living things with some kind of mentality exist in other worlds is now incontestable." I found this as amusing as another flat statement made by an evangelist I heard on our little battery radio this morning that "there is no question that Jesus rose from the dead because the Bible won't lie." Then I thought of biologists who were my university colleagues, working at least partially in the inner world of freedom and purpose, so glibly suggesting that we understand the causes of life, or are just about to understand them. And then I think of myself. Why do I, who cannot fathom his own mind, write about such dark problems as ethical and moral responsibility as I often do?

Faith in an open universe, while critical of dogmatism, wonderfully widens the field of the imaginatively possible for me. By a candid acceptance of rational opposites, it frees me to consider the most diverse explanations of things. I can at one time agree with Eddington that things never happen in the universe because they are too improbable, and at the same time believe in a destiny which is not determinism but time freed from the network of causal sequence. Or, as the trapper, who is my neighbor across two mountain passes would put it, "No matter what'cha do, you'll get yours when the time comes."

As I stepped outside the small cabin to again relieve myself and looked overhead to where numerous glittering stars appeared to spin around Polaris, I made my scientist's correction. It is the earth that spins. Then my colleague's question of years ago came back to me. "Do you believe in miracles?"

Tonight I can respond to his question with an affirming yes.

Life is the miracle. If it is the only miracle, it is enough. All the wonder stories and marvels of ancient gods and saviors bleach before the real miracle of life itself.

Tell me of virgin births and immaculate conceptions, or of Minerva springing from the forehead of Jove, or stones rolled from tombs, and I'll say that none of these compare with the germ of life, or those nine months while it is constantly changing, passing through eternal cycles of evolution to emerge into individual existence. Tell me of those mighty illuminations of the past: Of Zoroaster in the desert, of Buddha under the Bo tree, of Jesus on the mountain top, of Mohammed in his cave, and I'll say that none tells us more of ultimate reality than the gleam in a child's eye as she watches a butterfly settle on a flower, or stoops to examine a new litter of kittens.

Tell me of the resurrections of Tamuz, Adonis, Osiris, Jesus; and I'll say that every springtime holds equal glories of revived life forever being resurrected. That every cell of our own bodies is constantly undergoing renewal, that every electron and proton of what we used to call dead matter is teaming with incredible energy; that in each of us the very history of life is indelibly written.

This is our heritage, affirmed as the old is seen in a new way. Especially here tonight north of the Arctic Circle.

Homo Sapiens

He takes his life from other life,
the deepest meaning of original sin,
no chlorophyll,
and his stomach
will not ferment grass.

Yet he chuckles
    turning fruit into consciousness
    milk into songs,
    and meat into dreams
    that can build a new world.

A Polar Parable
Of the Bones of Fish

Now on a certain day the man of Koviashuvik and the woman of wisdom were invited to share repast with a catcher of fish.

And he who prepared the table before them, even a fish fry, did make much palaver about the savory char he had cooked.

Spake he much of the ways of fish and how to catch them. Moreover did he speak of the special way in which he prepared the lake trout for the table so that those who would partake should find no bones.

And the man of Koviashuvik and the woman of wisdom did partake of the savory dish, albeit not all of the bones had been removed.

Therein the man of Koviashuvik did place a bone on his plate wherein the woman of wisdom might see that it had not the straightness of the bones of the great char but was forked, even as the shape of a "Y."

And when they were apart from him who had prepared the meal, the woman of wisdom did speak to the man of Koviashuvik: "Peradventure we ate not trout but great northern pike, for the pike hath the Y bone."

And the man of Koviashuvik answered: "Yea, and not only the great northern pike. Another fish also hath the Y bone. The sucker!"

Then the woman of wisdom did look vexed and said: "Howbeit thou didst not speak?"

And the man of Koviashuvik answered her saying: "There are times when it is better to keep counsel. For as it is written of old: 'Even a fool, when he holdeth his peace, is counted wise; and he that shutteth his lips is esteemed a man of understanding.'"

Postscript

What we observe is not nature itself but nature exposed to our method of questioning.

—Werner Heisenberg

A silent world
in November.

November

THE SUN NO LONGER APPEARS above the jagged horizon. This morning the thermometer registered thirty degrees below zero as I stepped outside the cabin to lend my voice to the chorus of wolves singing on the hill above. As their howling died away, I was caught up and engulfed in the northern lights sweeping across the sky in great iridescent patterns like oil on the surface of water, but with the addition of three-dimensional depth.

South of the Arctic Circle and Yukon River, the Aurora Borealis is also a display of beauty. But here it is an experience for which there are no adequate words. It is somewhat like the light, motion, and forms sensed in the delirium of a high fever.

An Eskimo friend said that the old people call the Aurora "Spirit Light." I am aware of knowledge we now have about the cause of this phenomenon near outer space. However, there is a quality of experience here in which "Spirit Light" captures dimensions lost in the objective world of scientific description.

Over a mile away, across the lake, there are three graves. One is old John Rooney's, a prospector who died here in 1941. Another is the grave of Nakuchluk, the wife of Saukluk, or "Big Jim," one of the inland Eskimos who hunted and trapped here in the 1930s. The third gravesite holds the scattered ashes of Billie Wright, my former spouse of twenty years. On this day of the dead, snow blankets all beneath twisting colors of the aurora.

I mention these graves, where only a carved stone and a weathered wooden marker remain, because my adopted Eskimo grandmother said the old people called the northern lights "dancing souls of the dead." Tonight I know they are. I shouted out across the frozen lake, "Hey Rooney, Nakuchluk, and Billie, are you frozen in the grave or are you up there?"

The echo came back, "There."

Weather

With the disappearing sun, the cold of outer space once more reaches down through the clear arctic air to lock the range in silence.

In our snug cabin we put another log in the Yukon Stove and snuggle under the blankets on our spruce-pole bed to sip hot chocolate and listen to news through the static of our radio.

When the announcer reports blizzards in the midwest and a cold wave on the eastern seaboard, it is news of a friend from home.

An Arctic Allegory
Of That Which Giveth Offense

Now a certain man came to the far north that he might refresh himself away from the smog of the city. Peradventure to fish for lake trout and the great northern pike, also to breathe the clean air of wilderness.

Each day did he rise in the coolness of the early dawn and forthwith did he put on his jacket and take his rod to the shore to catch fish.

And as often as he returned to the cabin he did complain of the air, saying: "It stinketh of dead fish! The cabin needs be cleansed."

Now it also came to pass that on a certain day this man did wash his fishing jacket. And in so doing he turned outside the inside of the many pockets wherein he carried lures and lines and diverse things accumulated during many days.

And behold, a small dead fish did he find inside a waterproof pocket which had been placed there aforetimes for bait, albeit forgotten!

And when this was told to the man of Koviashuvik, he thought: "So it is with those who complain often of a stinking world while they carry with them that which giveth offense."

Beyond Death—Enigma of the Ages

Watching the northern lights swirl across the heavens north of the Arctic Circle, the Inuit Eskimo ask the same question as Job: "If a man die shall he live again?" This question has concerned people as far back as we can trace human history. Perhaps no question has intrigued humans more than the question of immortality.

I am also aware that for many this is a closed question. They neither accept nor reject personal immortality. They have no desire to reopen the question. This is because they have abandoned some earlier acceptance of what seemed an irrational acceptance or consideration of personal immortality. Their reasoning goes something like this: Birth, growth, decline, and death of the body; of animals as well as humans, is an inescapable phenomenon. Without a brain there can be no thoughts. When the brain dies and disintegrates, thoughts die and therefore the mind dies. Consequently, that which is uniquely me—my personality, mind, soul—ceases to be.

A case is often made about a person continuing as a physical being in her or his child, but the child is a new and different personality. It is also true that a person's deeds and actions live on in the deeds and actions of posterity, particularly through those people with whom we come into direct contact. However, the question of individual immortality is for many a closed question. But for those who have personal and immediate contact with the land and the world of nature, the question is always open.

❧

In using a word like soul, I need to define the term. I refer to that, which out of the billions of people on earth, we designate as "I." Is this strangely unique self which seems to inhabit your and my physical body destined to die? Whether we like it or not, sooner or later, in some hospital room, or on the pavement of some highway, or in swirling waves or the cold, or in bed at home, our bodies will go limp for the last time. Our hearts will cease to pump blood to our brain. Our bodies will be dead.

But what of that strange uniqueness that has said "I" within each of our bodies all these years? Will it also flicker out like a burned-out candle? Or will that selfhood which some call soul go on into wider worlds or into vaster adventures?

A variety of methods have been used in seeking answers to the question of life after death. All are ultimately based on the historical and cultural context of the seeker.

Some quote the Bible or the Koran or other sacred texts as their authority. Some philosophers seek to prove life beyond death by abstract logic. And there are those who use poetry and literary eloquence in setting forth their own inner intuitive assurance of life beyond death, such as spirits dancing in the aurora. However, neither arbitrary authority, nor logic, nor unsupported intuition will serve the need for many minds that seek answers to the enigma of the ages.

∽

In the world of science there are those who have disposed of the continuity of the soul by the simple assertion that only the sensory-motor world is real. If the concept of soul exists at all, it functions in a world of consciousness and purpose.

Experiments, of which I was once a part, have placed people in so-called sensory-free environments, much like being deep in a cavern or mine without light or sound. There, comfortably relaxed, we could approach fairly closely for the time being an exclusion of the sensory-motor world of sight, touch, smell, taste, hearing, and movement. I could still remain conscious, remember the past and plan for the future. I could still imagine, dream, think through the multiplication table, or engage in abstract reasoning. Although my motor senses were more or less inactive, there remained the world of memory, planning, imagination, dreams, abstract thought, and imageless intuition.

I became aware that this concept of soul, or self, functions in the world of consciousness and purpose. So the question becomes whether or not the focus of consciousness can observe and operate apart from the physical body?

Whether one accepts the findings or not, carefully controlled experiments have been made in so-called extra-sensory perception at distances ranging from a quarter of a mile to thousands, and there seemed to be no relationship between distance and success. The assumptions made from this was that minds, under certain circumstances, observe what occurs in other minds away from the physical body of the observer. Therefore, the focus of consciousness of certain persons appeared to observe at a distance from the physical body in ways not yet understood. For some, this lays the foundation for acceptance of some form of belief in a separate soul.

Based on these kinds of experimental research, the soul or self has been defined operationally as that portion or aspect of a personality that can observe and operate apart from its physical body. The operational test of the existence of such a self consists in determining by experimentation whether the focus of consciousness can make its presence, ideas, and images known apart from the physical body. However, saying that evidence points to the reality of a soul that can operate at a distance from the physical body is not the same as saying that the soul can observe and operate after its physical body has been destroyed. It is the question of survival after the death of the body that is Job's question.

∾

If the self can in some cases escape the physical body and observe at a distance what is happening and what other people are thinking, this is disturbing to our ordinary ideas of reality. But there is a still more disturbing observation current, which is that consciousness not only appears to transcend space, but also transcends time. In some strange sense, the future is already in existence.

I recall an Eskimo shaman in a deep trance telling us of his vision of caribou crossing the mountains north of the village during the next two days. The following morning hunters left and met the herd as he foretold. I accused the shaman, who was a friend of mine, of just making an educated guess based upon his hunting experience. He laughed and said his guesses were no better than anybody else's. He said he had been wrong many times, but the visions in his trance had never failed. "Ask anyone in the village," he said. I did. They confirmed him.

This phenomenon occurs not just among the shaman of the Eskimo. People under experimental conditions are reported to have slipped into the future and perceived events in detail that later took place as they had been foreseen. If the generally accepted precognition data are valid, they force us to do a great deal of rethinking our view of reality. Our physical personalities appear to be vehicles through which our real selves experience the drama called life. If this is so, then death in our physical world cannot extinguish the essential selfhood which says "I" in us. Our existence then appears to be beyond both the space and time of earth.

This is still heresy to those who proclaim that personality is only the expression of the physical body with its organs, its muscles, and glands, based on the reality of the material world with its physical space, measured by the surveyor's tape, and time measured by the swing of material planets and the tick of brass clock wheels.

Even in physics, and especially there, the materialistic theory of existence is on the defensive. Today, the old materialistic view of reality is no longer supportable by the weight of evidence.

∾

Tonight, beneath the swirls of the aurora on this Day of the Dead, which follows All Hallow's Eve with its ghosts and goblins, Job's ancient question comes in a new context of how we conceive the universe and our role in it.

First, from a subatomic perspective, this universe appears to be immaterial. The classic word is spiritual, from the concept of essence or breath. Matter consists of the rigorous outworkings of the patterns by which spirit acts and builds. We live and move and have our being within a greater relationship or entity.

Second, our life here on earth appears to be a drama taking place within this universal spirituality. As one great writer put it: Our immortal spirits are actors cast in the roles of a divine comedy.

Third, death is our final exit in the character we have been playing in the present act. As for others who have made their exit called death, some still challenge our earth-bound personalities to look up and out beyond the stars, and in our deepest hearts we hold communion with those who have gone before.

And fourth, being privileged, for a little while, to move about on the stage of creative life, let us explore reality reverently and courageously, knowing that our destiny reaches far beyond the scenery, the make-up, and the properties of this present stage of experience.

There is no partisan view of immortality that has a corner on emotional satisfaction. There is as much deep feeling in reflection on human mortality as immortality.

I conclude that the calm facing of one's own death has little to do with the professions of belief or disbelief in immortality. What seems to count most is the ability to remove death from the category of things evil to the category of things natural. It is the wonder of human life that it can be extinguished and even forgotten and still go on influencing the living world forever after. For many this is the only immortality. For me it is enough.

Eternity

We live in eternity.
Yesterday I died
Because yesterday is gone
And will be no more.
How many times I die!
This moment passed
is gone,
'Twill be no more than a dream.
But I am in eternity,
And each moment is a time of birth,
The joy of new experience
Of work and play and rest.
Who knows what tomorrow
holds.

Is the hope of immortality in the
birth
Of new experience?
An experience
Called death.

A Polar Parable
Of Moose Scats in the Snow

Now it came to pass that the man of Koviashuvik and the woman of wisdom did sojourn to a strange country, even among them that dwell in the lower forty-eight.

There, in a great city, they did fall in with diverse men and women of affairs. And these did talk of nothing except troubles. Spake they of the hair and dress of their children and how students no longer accept the wisdom of their forebears or the learning of the sages in the great university. Moreover did they speak exceedingly of money and taxes and of great tribulations even as Medes and Persians who respecteth not the true faith.

Amongst the palaver, the man of Koviashuvik joined not in the talk concerning these troubles. Kept he his mouth shut lest his ignorance be clearly revealed unto others.

Then did one of the men of affairs inquire of him saying: "Hast thou great tribulation concerning these diverse things?"

And the man of Koviashuvik answered: "Nay, none whatsoever."

Then the men and women of affairs were amazed and inquired of him what the nature of his business might be. And he answered them saying: "The woman of wisdom and I dwell in a far place where we observe. This is our business."

Then they asked of him: "What observest thou in such a business?"

And he answered them, saying: "We have learned that hours and days falleth like moose scats in the snow, which in the spring are swept by mighty waters to the sea from whence they return no more."

Postscript

Philosophy begins in wonder, and at the end, when philosophy has done its best, the wonder remains.

—Alfred North Whitehead

*A full moon
for Christmas.*

December

THIS GIANT BALL on which we live appears to come to a grinding halt in late December. I can almost feel the adjustment of billions of tons of mountains, seas, and molten rock shuddering to a stop before reversing themselves to tip back toward the sun of summer.

Actually, this spinning earth does not tip. Its axis, from pole to pole, slants so that our yearly orbit around the sun gives us this grand illusion.

The sun has disappeared from view for more than a month. Stars appear at two o'clock in the afternoon. It is easy to understand why primal people developed rituals to return the sun at this winter solstice.

From now on, days will become longer. Slowly at first, just a few minutes a day. By early February the sun will have returned. In the middle of June, the sun will not set but move around the sky and dip briefly behind a mountain peak on the horizon at midnight. Discounting the clouds, every place on earth gets the same amount of sunlight. Here, north of the Arctic Circle, it is dramatically distributed from sunless winter days to summer's midnight sun.

This seems to be the context for everything here in this northern mountain wilderness. Dramatic.

Drama is one of the reasons for its appeal to adventurous spirits. Like the drama of the great grey wolves whose howls, as they gather at the site of a caribou kill, echo and re-echo through the foothills. Or the caribou themselves, with their four to five foot sweep of antlers, which dramatize their elegance in their migration through the range in great herds.

Even the small twelve by twelve foot cabin has a dramatic perch high on a mountain shelf, hundreds of feet above the deep lake. The mountains add their drama, with Mount Truth jutting up 3,000 feet above the cabin. And above all is the great dome of sky with its sweep of color, clouds, and northern lights.

Here, at the turn of the year, all seems larger and clearer—a reminder that life is everywhere adventuresome and dramatic, if we could better learn to see.

Weather

Temperatures begin to level off in December well below the zero mark. The air becomes noticeably dryer.

Although direct sunlight disappeared in November, daylight still reddens the sky at mid-day with a color combination of sunrise and sunset. Stars appear by 2:30 in the afternoon. It is a quiet time of year. Snow drifts very little because there is seldom any wind.

Snowshoeing a trail several miles up the mountainside to where I had stacked a teepee of dead trees in the fall, I was interested in checking the limitations of working in the cold.

It was only thirty-two degrees below zero on the cabin thermometer when I left, but there was an unusual breeze blowing. The chill factor was about sixty degrees below zero.

At this time of year the cold is a relationship of many factors, not just the measure on a thermometer. One important element is the speed of the wind, expressed as chill factor.

In mid-winter I find that as long as I keep my nose and cheeks protected by a face mask behind the wolverine fur of my parka when facing the wind, I can avoid frostbite. I am also careful not to expose fingers except briefly. The major problem is to avoid sweating from the effort of snowshoeing in deepening snow. When perspiration freezes, chilling is unavoidable. Well-ventilated clothing is necessary even in the coldest weather.

An Arctic Allegory
Of Speaking With the Voice of Thunder

Now the man of Koviashuvik was sorely troubled for he found not a last chapter to his tale.

During the long night of winter did he read many books and magazines, those of murder and detectives that had been flown in aforetimes. Even those stories with many clues and diverse suspects. And here cometh a tale from which the end hath been torn asunder.

Then spake he aloud in a voice of thunder to the woman in the cabin saying: "Who teareth out the end of this tale?" And he looked at her with an eye to terrify a great moose or even the mighty grizzly bear.

Only then did he remember that it was he who had torn out pages to kindle a morning fire in the Yukon Stove. Peradventure he was thinking not with clarity in the early dawn.

Then did he humble himself and pondered in his heart: "When we speak to others in a loud voice of authority it is most often ourselves who should hear."

Wolverine

I discovered the moose just before freezeup, floating in six feet of water about twenty yards offshore. His great rack of antlers held him like an anchor to the bottom in the shallows north of Caribou Island. His hindquarter floated above the surface only a day or two before the ice locked his body in place for the winter. How he had died, I could not tell. No external signs of injury from wolves were visible. He might have been hurt internally in battle with another bull during rut, and in the shallows off the lake shore had drowned.

I had visited the moose several times to see if wolves had discovered it, but it remained untouched until a wolverine found the carcass after snows had covered the protruding haunch.

This is still the wilderness of the timber wolf, the grizzly bear, and the epitome of wildness, "carcajou," as the Algonquian Indians and French trappers called him—the wolverine.

I watched the wolverine as he tore at the moose carcass. His movements were quick. He would rise above the surrounding snow, look sharply left and right, then circle around to tear at the meat from the opposite side.

Moving downwind, I snowshoed into the trees of the island in order to approach the feeding animal without being seen. Recalling stories of the ferocity and fearlessness of this giant member of the weasel family, I threw a cartridge into the breech of my rifle as I eased up to look over a snowdrift on the island shore.

I could see nothing move in the white hollow where the carcass was exposed. He had gone. Then, in the distance, I sighted the dark figure crossing the lake toward the opposite shore, loping through the snow in his characteristic crab-like gait.

Seeing a wolverine in his native environment is an uncommon experience. Naturalist Earnest Thompson Seton reported sighting only two in his lifetime. Except for the wolverine's longer flexible neck, he might be mistaken at a distance for a brown bear cub, or, if he were not so agile, for a porcupine. He seldom weighs more than forty pounds but he has a reputation among northern trappers as the most ferocious animal in the Brooks Range. Part of his reputation no doubt comes from the voracious appetite which has given him his name, "Gulo gulo," the glutton.

Late one autumn I cached nearly 200 bounds of bear meat high in a spruce tree. An early snowstorm prevented my returning for several days. When I did get back, only one well-gnawed bone remained on the ground beneath the tree. Claw marks on the bark, tracks on the ground, and musk odor in the area were unmistakably wolverine. The glutton must have had help, but there was no sign of any other animal.

The wolverine, called the devil of the woods by trappers, has been known to follow a trapline for miles, eating every animal caught and springing empty traps as if for spite.

Widely distributed in the arctic and subarctic, wolverines are not abundant, although a neighbor in Wiseman trapped several last winter. This was an unusual catch; the world's annual harvest of wolverine pelts is only about 1,000.

Wolverine fur is considered the finest for ruffs on winter parkas. Eskimos use it to trim the part that contacts the face because the fur does not mat or freeze to the skin when the temperature drops to fifty or sixty below zero. I now have a prime wolverine pelt acquired under circumstances in which the moose, frozen in the ice, played a role.

The wolverine lives alone except during the short mating period in the spring and for a few months following birth in a hillside den in early June. The two or three cubs are given a brief course in hunting by their mother during the short summer and are abandoned in the fall. Solitary, intelligent, and self-reliant, the wolverine roams the northern mountains in harmony with other creatures, endangered only when confronting the values of humans. If people ever tame the wolverine, something important will have disappeared from the earth.

I had not visited the moose carcass for several weeks. It was twenty below zero, and the day before Christmas. With our beagle pup, "Girl," I snowshoed across the frozen lake. Three feet of snow covered the ice and Girl would bound ahead and leap up above the white cover in order to see. When she tired, or when I called her to heel, she would drop behind my snowshoes to follow where I had already broken trail.

Girl was given to me shortly before she had been weaned, and after nine months she was nearly grown but still had her puppy enthusiasm. She had become an intimate part of our wilderness life— I thought of her more in human terms than as another animal.

Girl and I crossed the lake to check my snares on the far side. We started back shortly after noon so we would not be caught by dark. With the sun's return still a month away, even at midday the winter gloom limited visibility. At sub-zero temperatures, watery eyes and frosted eyelashes added to the limitations.

I decided to return by way of the island to see if any animal had fed on the remains of the moose, and was within a hundred feet before I saw a dark head rise above the white expanse. Girl, jumping through the snow in front of me, saw it at the same time. She raced ahead with great leaps.

The wolverine, not much larger than the dog, immediately left the hollow where he had been feeding on the moose and galloped toward the island. I believe Girl thought she had discovered a playmate, for she paid no attention to my sharp call to stay, but bounded after him. In the wolverine's track, she gained distance rapidly, ignoring my shouts.

When she was within ten feet of the animal, what happened took place so quickly that I am not sure of the details. But it appeared that the wolverine whirled about, throwing himself on his back. Girl's momentum was so great she could not stop. There was a snarling jumble of bodies, a shrill, piercing cry, and the wolverine continued on into the trees of the island.

Instinctively I had thrown a cartridge into the breech of my .22 rifle. When I reached Girl, I put her out of her misery without hesitation. She had been ripped open by the slashing claws, and badly torn by the sharp teeth.

With loaded gun, I followed the wolverine's tracks through the trees and across the island to where they continued out onto the lake ice. In the distance I watched the bobbing dark spot disappear into the twilight.

Returning to Girl's body with its red stain in the snow, I carried her remains to the island. Everything was frozen solid; it was impossible to bury her. The wolverine would certainly be back.

There is an unbroken circle in life and death like the hoop of the steel snare I took from my pack after placing the dog's body in a hollow at the base of a dwarf spruce tree. I set the snare with care and snowshoed to the cabin alone as the aurora danced across the sky.

The next day I returned to the island. I was met by deep, hoarse growls. The wolverine was caught around the waist by the snare. If it had not been strong steel, securely wired around a spruce tree, the snare would never have held him. He had chewed off all the branches within reach, leaving an open area the length of the tether. There was no sign of Girl's remains. On my approach, his fierce snarls, grunts, and rushes were so violent that for a moment I was concerned that he might snap the steel leash and be on me. Never have I seen such fury and fearlessness in a creature. Although he was my victim he gave the impression that the situation was reversed.

A beautiful animal, he was heavily muscled, with broad, almost golden stripes on either side accenting the thick dark fur on his back. I considered releasing him. He was unharmed, and it was Christmas day, but there was no way to approach him without endangering myself or badly injuring him.

And so I acquired a prime wolverine pelt for my parka. I am not at all certain of the value of the exchange.

To Know the Difference

This morning the mid-winter stillness was broken by the call of a raven. His call reminded me that among the Indians of the northwest coast, the coming of death is recognized when a raven calls your name. Fortunately, he did not call mine. As I watched the black silhouette soar against the grey sky of December, I thought of life and death and anniversaries.

This is the annual tip of the northern end of the earth, promising a return of the sunny days of summer. The raven reminds me that December is also the anniversary of the birth of human flight.

The significance of this birth has meaning for us here in our isolation, as we are more dependent upon the airplane than many. The birth of human flight was no minor happening. Like other firsts, something new arrived that changed the world.

It was in December of 1903 that Orville Wright crawled to his prone position between the wings of the biplane he and his brother Wilbur had built, opened the throttle of their homemade twelve horsepower engine, and took to the air. He covered 120 feet in twelve seconds. Later that day in one of four flights, Wilbur stayed up fifty-nine seconds and covered 852 feet. I have friends with living relatives who were around at that time, but legends have already begun to separate facts and fiction.

From this point in time I would not venture to predict what meaning the birth of human flight might have in the future. There are no blazed trails to meaning. Trails are made in the traveling.

Other December anniversaries, such as Christmas and Hanukkah, go back to a time far distant from us and the anniversaries which preceded them back to the dim origins of an almost immemorial past. These have become legends in which the facts, as we think of them today, have been transformed into significant meanings. They are no longer history. They do not deal with facts, but in them sing the subjective truths that have sung in people's hearts for centuries, and which find a sympathetic echo in our own, at this time of year.

This is the way it is in December with the Christmas birth stories. They are not history. They do not deal with facts, but in them is great beauty and meaning. They are legends which mean little to us in terms of reasoned fact. An attempt to see what historical facts they yield produces very little. However, this search for historical facts has been done by scholars and students of history.

As a matter of fact, we find that it is highly improbable that Jesus was born in Bethlehem at all. The Hebrew prophets had dreamed of a deliverer, a messiah, a king, who would be born in

Bethlehem, the alleged birthplace of David. A deliverer, who would drive out the foreigners and reestablish a Jewish kingdom.

The early Christians and converted Jews tried to identify Jesus with this Jewish national hope. So the legend grew that Jesus was born in Bethlehem rather than Nazareth. Also that Joseph, his mother's husband, was of the royal family.

As a matter of fact, his family was of humble origin. Also, as a matter of fact, Jews did not have to go to the birthplace of their ancestors to register, as the legend says. According to the chronology accepted by most scholars as the best biblical chronology, Cyrenius was not governor when Jesus was born and there was no registration until 6 AD. As a matter of fact, virgins do not have babies. As a matter of fact, stars do not and can not behave as one did in the story of the Magi. As a matter of fact, wise men would know that. As a matter of fact, there are no angels. As a matter of fact, the message the legend says they delivered would be incomprehensible to the shepherds of that time. As a matter of fact, such a message would have paralyzed them with fear and they never would have remembered the poem that the legend says they heard.

To believe these fancies to be facts is to indulge in superstition. But if we know that this is not history, but legend, we can see the beautiful poetry in it all.

The mystery captivates us. We love these stories beyond others. They are some of the first we read to our children. They sing their way into our hearts and drive out misery. They are the carrier of meanings by which we measure nations. They are not objective facts like the machine which carried Orville and Wilbur Wright into the air, or the height and depth of the ebb and flow of the tide. Instead they have subjective meanings, poetic truths that have sung in people's hearts for centuries.

To know the difference between subjective truth and fact, to be able to see truth within a legend or myth, is one of the greatest gifts life can bestow.

A friend of mine once put it this way: "I know there is a Santa Claus. I don't have to reason about it. I know it by feeling. Voltaire said that if there were no God it would be necessary to invent one. That's what happened. There was no Santa Claus, so some genius, some unknown child-loving priest or prelate, invented one. I've known Santa all my life. He was a friend of my father's and of his father; and my mother and her mother and her mother. He has always been a friend of our family. He is as real to me as any of my brothers and sisters. Why, in our family he is the first stranger to whom we introduce our babies. He is practically a member of the family. Old St. Nick, I guess, is the only saint we ever had in our family. I know him intimately. I have done business with him. I have known of his work all my days and I call that work good. Why, he has taken trouble and disappointment and transformed it into a most blessed Christmas. Of course he is not an objective fact like a building or tree, but he is a truth, a glorious, rollicking, heart-lifting, gloom-dispelling, poetic truth! Fie on these dyspeptic, watery-veined old grouches who go around telling little girls and boys, 'They ain't no Santy Claus!'"

This turn of the year, this anniversary of another cycle around the sun, reminds me that feeling, imagination, and wonder are as much a part of reality as the fire in the Yukon Stove which warms our cabin tonight. Perhaps even more so.

There are emotional needs which have been ours since before the dawn of history. They are sometimes very subtle, and are denied at the cost of spiritual death. They are marked by such different words as "adventure" and "solitude." There is a restlessness and impatience with things as they are which the distractions and comforts of modern life do not satisfy.

For more than a million years we have lived with the seasons, the flow of water, the rising and setting of the sun, the migrations of herds, the turn of stars around the sky. In wilderness there is an ancient rhythm, an insight into the meaning of life and death, where we find roots deep in the soil of ancient experience when life seemed simple and satisfactions real.

I sought that experience in this northern wilderness, to learn what it had to teach, and found its lessons encompassed in this year around the sun. But the earth does not pause. It has already swung into another year, another time, and another journey.

And so, as Thoreau wrote in *Walden*: "I left the woods for as good a reason as I went there. Perhaps it seemed to me that I had several more lives to live, and could not spare any more time for that one. It is remarkable how easily and insensibly we fall into a particular route, and make a beaten track for ourselves. I had not lived there a week before my feet wore a path from my door to the pond side. The surface of the earth is soft and impressible by the feet of men; and so with the paths the mind travels. How worn and dusty, then, must be the ruts of tradition and conformity. I did not wish to take a cabin passage, but rather to go before the mast and on the deck of the world, for there I could best see the moonlight amid the mountains."

To Speak Truth With Love

In my view from the top of the world
　　There is an inherent conflict
　　Between truth and love.
It is true that "there ain't no Santy Claus,"
　　But in love
　　I would not knowingly
　　Shatter a child's dreams.
And that's the truth!

Truth stands off in silence
　　Across the lake,
A jagged peak
　　That thrusts into a blue which
　　Sings of northern lights
　　And sparkling snow.

Because of love
　　I bite my tongue a thousand times and do not say,
　　"That isn't true."
And in the sin of silence
　　Lie and cheat.
To speak the truth is shattered dreams.

Truth stands bold and clean against the sky.
　　And blue is true,
　　Or is it only a rhyme
　　Like love above?
In love I would be silent.
In truth I would speak.

A Polar Parable
Of Lowlands and Mountains

Now in the days that are remembered there dwelt a people in the lowlands.

And it came to pass, after they had labored throughout the winter months and done all their work, they went forth unto the high mountains that rise above the plains.

And the mountains were to the weary and heavy-laden a place of vision. There did their spirits rise like eagles. From the heights they beheld the world afresh. There they saw afar, peradventure a vision that overcometh heavy burdens of the lowlands.

Howsoever, there were others in the lowlands that came not to the mountains. Neither did they understand those who did journey there. And among those who journeyed not, some did complain exceedingly of the burdens of the lowlands. Even so, they lifted not their eyes unto the hills.

And so it was that there were those who lived and died in the lowlands. There they were gathered unto their mothers and fathers never having seen the mysteries that were revealed to others. And thus it did appear that none could tell them so they might understand.

The man of Koviashuvik did ponder this and thinketh to himself: "So it has ever been. There seems no way to reveal a vision unto them who seek it not."

Postscript

Tomorrow is a day of watching and waiting. We never know exactly when we might be picked up by the bush plane. Before leaving we prearranged a date for pickup but months have passed and plans in the pilot's family schedule may have been changed and weather may be intervening.

Yesterday was a day of organizing departure. Leaving in winter takes time. Putting away bedding in barrels, covering windows as protection from bears, then waiting a half mile from our winter cabin in a shelter near the shore where we can stay warm while listening for the plane to land on our frozen lake. We must be ready to leave immediately. Bush planes do not shut down in frigid arctic temperatures.

Since the plane didn't arrive by early afternoon we expect there was not enough light left today to come and return to Fairbanks. So it was back up the hill to uncover a window, rekindle the fire, take bedding from barrels, search the cache for something for supper. Our cabin warmed quickly as it has only had a few hours with no fire. I fry mooseburgers. We toast the future in tiny jelly glasses saved for special occasions and as we sit in the glow of our Yukon Stove, speculate about what tomorrow may bring.

—Woman of Wisdom (from her journal)

This journey around the sun ends near the top of the world. However, a journey around the sun would end near the bottom of the earth if we turned our globes and atlases upside down.

We are supported by structures of the past to which we have become accustomed, while a new age is rising all around us. It is the edge of tomorrow which beckons us to see beyond wherever we are.

—Man of Koviashuvik

About the Author

BORN IN THE MINING CAMP of Santa Rita, New Mexico, Sam Wright grew up among miners, cowboys, and Indians and follows a life perspective he calls "an adventure in the exploration of meaning." After two years away at prep school, Wright returned to the Southwest to earn degrees in biology and anthropology from the University of New Mexico and became a teaching fellow there before being drafted into service during World War II. After the war, he taught biological sciences at the University of Texas in El Paso and then earned a graduate degree in theology at a seminary in Berkeley, California, where he later held a full professorship.

During a sabbatical leave in 1968, Sam and his new wife, Billie, moved into the wilderness of Alaska north of the Arctic Circle. There they built a twelve-foot by twelve-foot log cabin with simple hand tools on a slope above a mountain lake. Their goal was to experience intimately the traditional Eskimo way of life by emulating it as much as possible. Billie Wright's award-winning book, *Four Seasons North: A Journal of Life in the Alaskan Wilderness*, was her account of their first year in the cabin which they named Koviashuvik, an Eskimo word for "living in the present moment with quiet joy and happiness." Billie died in December 1987 and asked for her ashes to be scattered at Koviashuvik.

In 1988, Sam Wright published *Koviashuvik* with Sierra Club Books as the second volume in their new library of nature and nature philosophy. The University of Arizona Press reissued *Koviashuvik* in 1997.

Wright and his new wife, Donna Lee, currently divide their time between Alaska and Arizona.